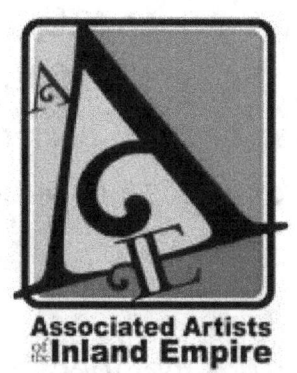

Associated Artists
of Inland Empire

THE ASSOCIATED ARTISTS OF THE INLAND EMPIRE

THE AAIE
COLORING BOOK

Who Are We?

Associated Artists of the Inland Empire (AAIE) was established in 1964 and held the first Membership art show in the spring of that year. In the years since its beginning, the purpose of AAIE has been to promote the creative talent of its members, to provide an exchange of ideas between area artists, and to generate public interest in fine arts.

AAIE has grown from a few dedicated members to a current enrollment of about 250 artists. New members are accepted on an ongoing basis. Membership is open to artists of all levels of accomplishment, and to those working in any media. The only requirement for membership is a genuine interest in creating or sharing the enjoyment of artwork.

Monthly meetings are held the second Wednesday of each month at 9:30 a.m. at the Goldy S. Lewis Community Center, 11200 Baseline Road, Rancho Cucamonga, California. Well-known, talented artists are invited to demonstrate in a variety of media at each monthly general meeting. The demonstrations are open to the public. Members are advised by a monthly newsletter of art-related events from our area and throughout Southern California. An Annual Juried Art Show allows members to compete with one another and with artists from other areas.

The meetings and yearly show keep members abreast of a variety of techniques and of what is happening in the art techniques and of what is happening in the art community. At the same time, AAIE hopes to make the community more familiar with art and local artists

Please visit our website: **associatedartistsinlandempire.org**

The Contributing Member Artists

(in alphabetical order)

The artist's name is on the <u>BACK</u> of each image in the book

Shirley Bonneville
Nancy Brinkley
Dorothy Campbell
Rita Cavin
Karen Clark
Carolyn Cunningham
Cindee J. Dunlap
Lynn Fearman
Alma Ford
Sandi Grimley
Charlene Hobbs
Jan Hydeman
NancyKasten
Keith Klingonsmith
Sarah Kowalski
Tess Lee
Deannie Laughrun
J. Lea
Ellen De Lorm
Fran Ortiz
Joan Robben
Robin Rollins
Mark Rush
Maris Sherwood
J. Steffens
Ray Tucker
Lorna Vacarri
Erma Williams

The Coloring Book Phenomena

Adult Coloring books have become a popular trend throughout the world. This trend has no intention of slowing down either. Adult coloring books offer the individual a wonderful way to pass the time and reap some very valuable mental and physical benefits. Coloring lowers one's blood pressure, reduces stress, helps to maintain your cognitive skills , develops your attention and focus. Most important it's just plain fun!

AAIE invites you to get out your favorite color pencils, markers or whatever medium you fancy and get creative.

Proceeds from the sale of this coloring book goes towards the AAIE scholarship program which benefits both AAIE members and young artists of our surrounding communities.

Thank you for your purchase and now ……….. start coloring!

PLEASE NOTE:

When coloring the images it is best to put another sheet of heavier paper behind it to protect the following image from being damaged.

Color pencils do work the best. Use, if possible, an artist's brand of pencil such as those produced by Prisma (available at art and craft stores). Professional quality pencils are much more pigmented and produce rich, vibrant colors. Color markers tend to bleed through the paper. They are not advised.

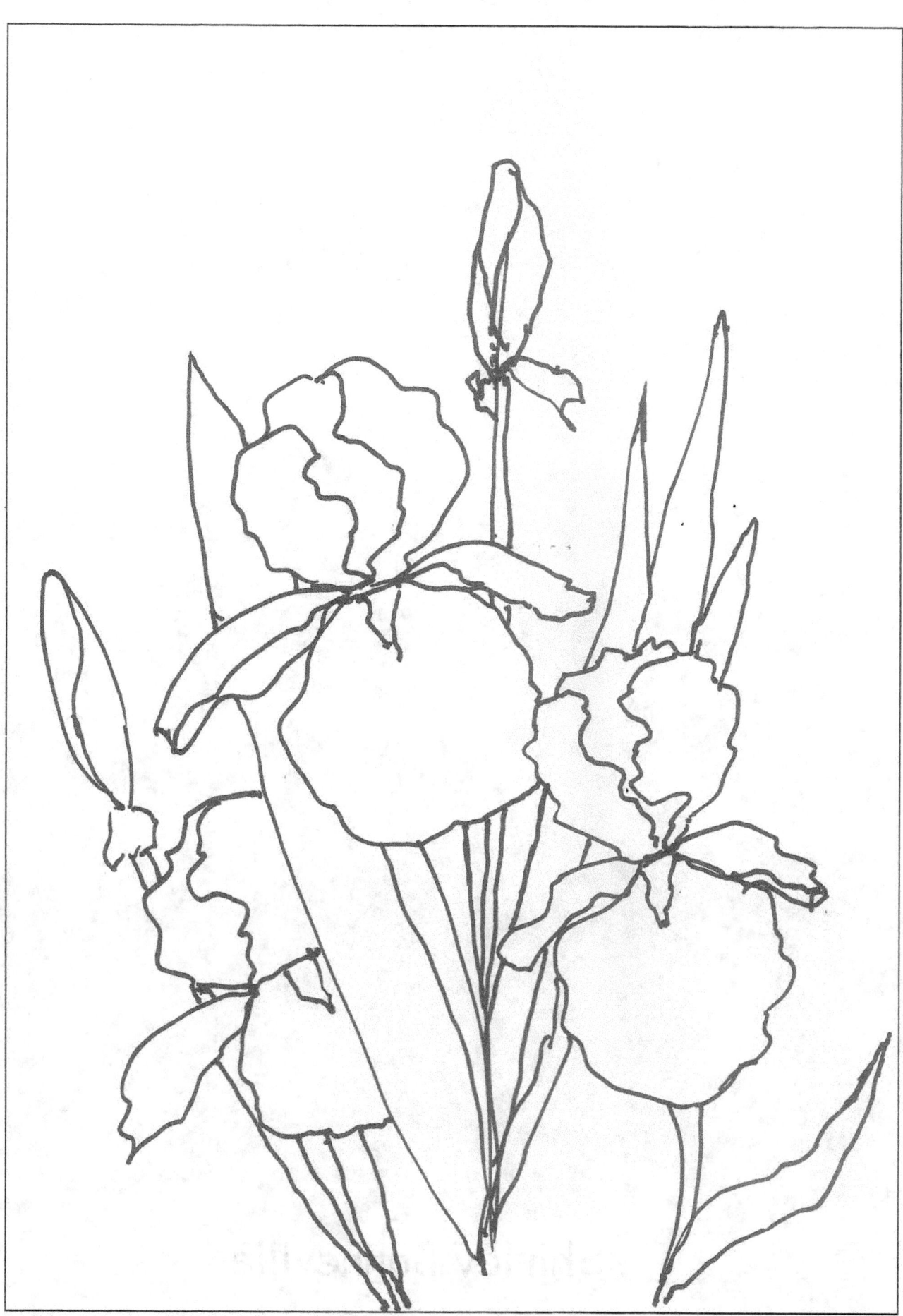

Shirley Bonneville

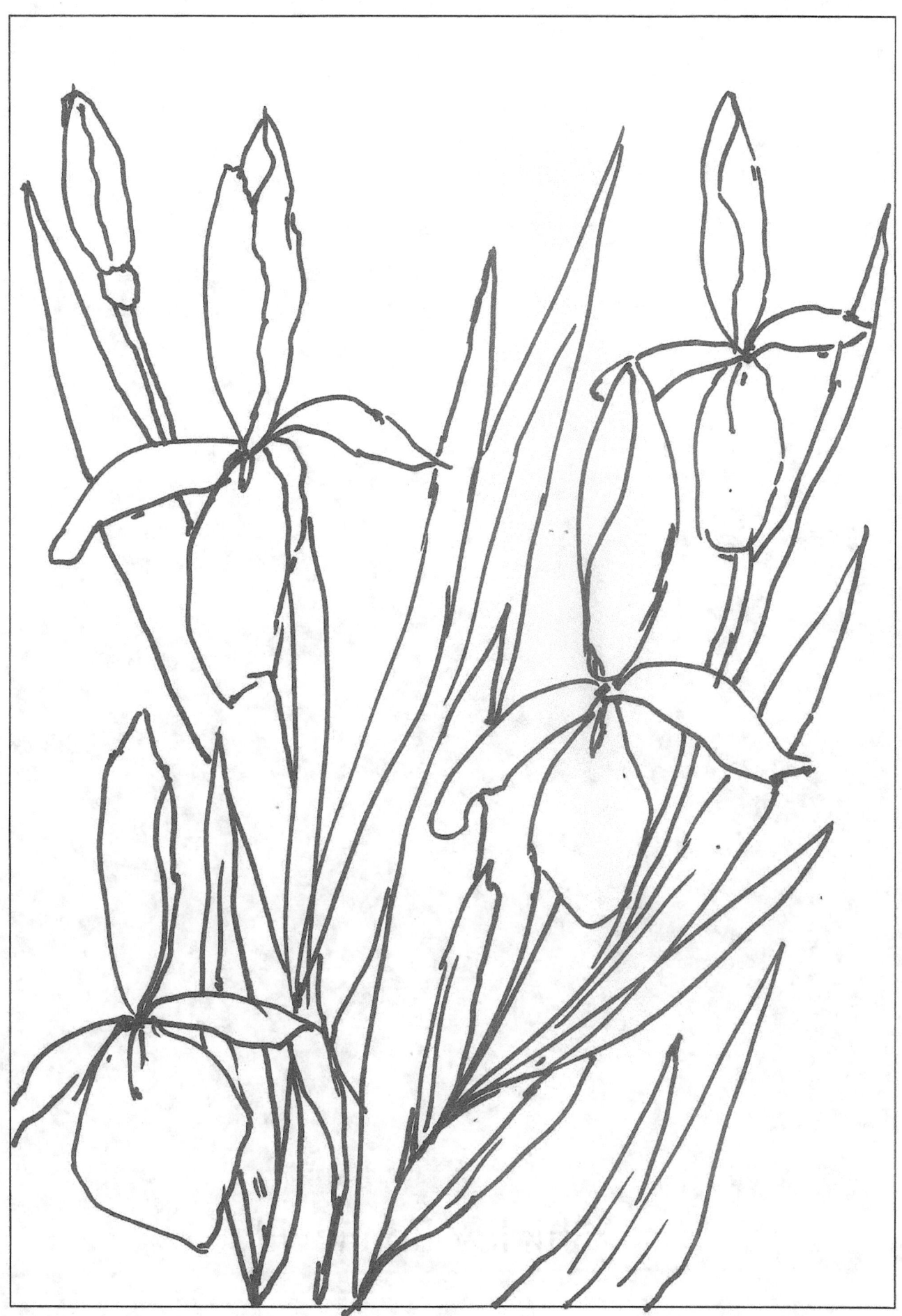

Shirley Bonneville

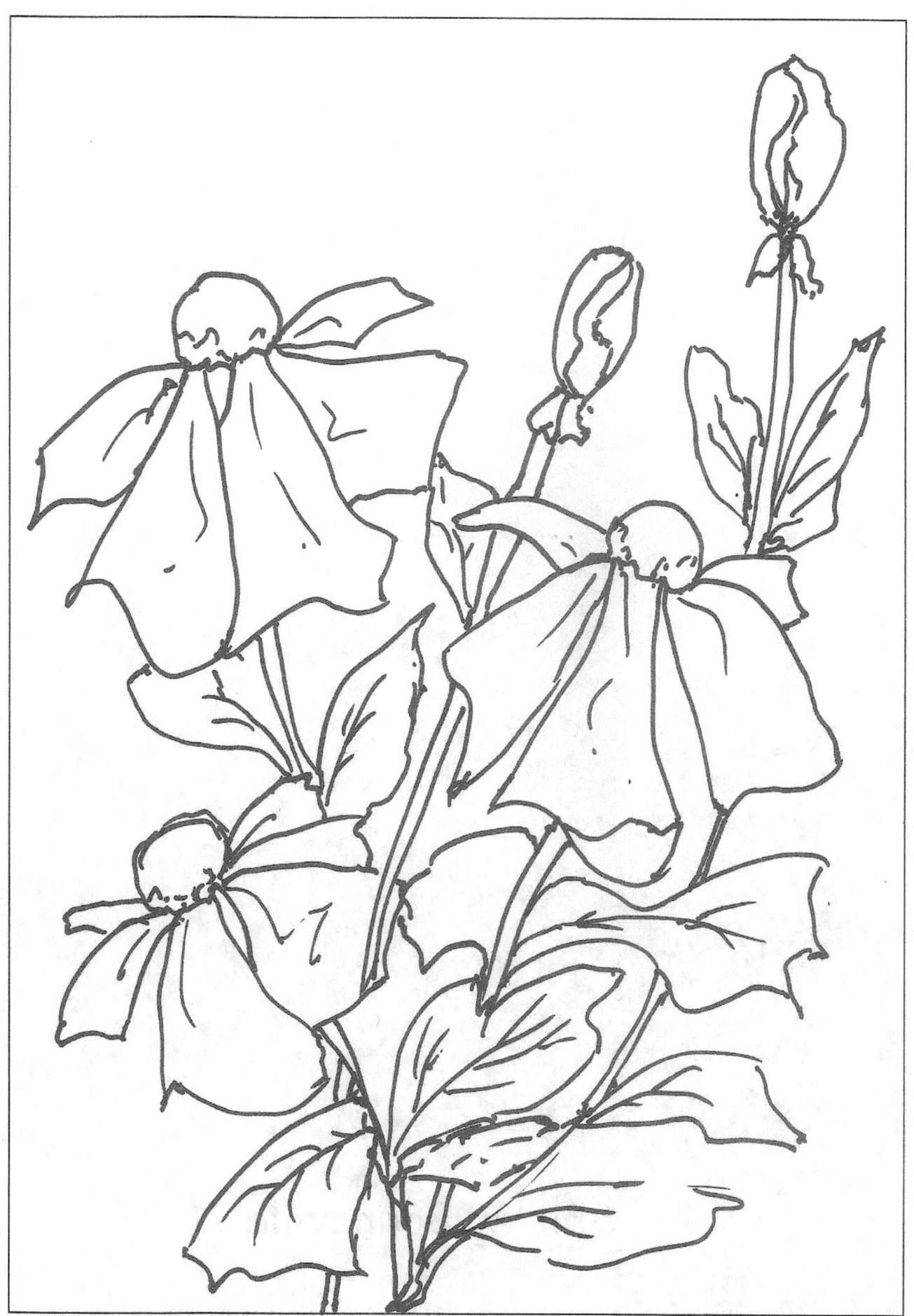

Shirley Bonneville

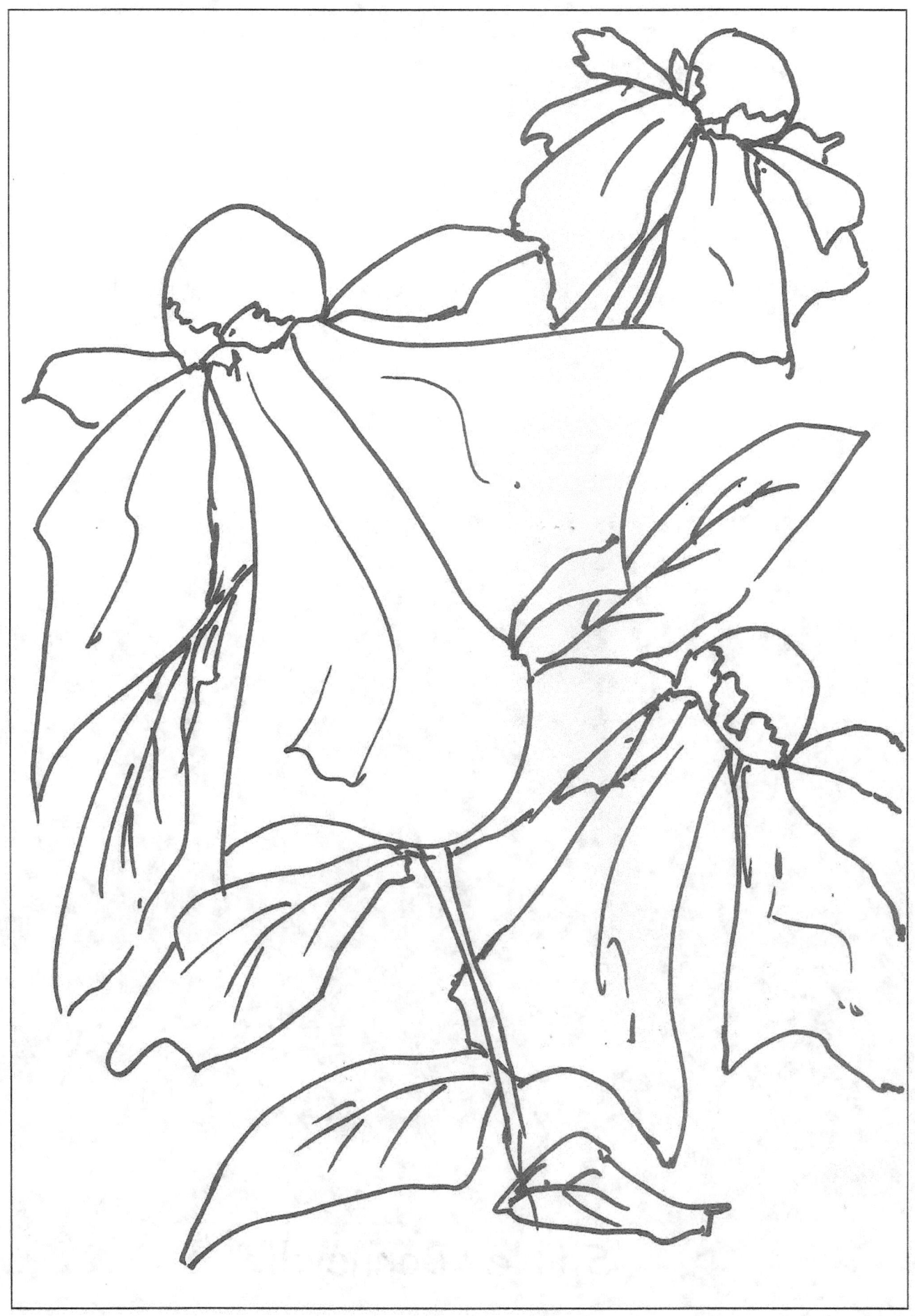

Shirley Bonneville

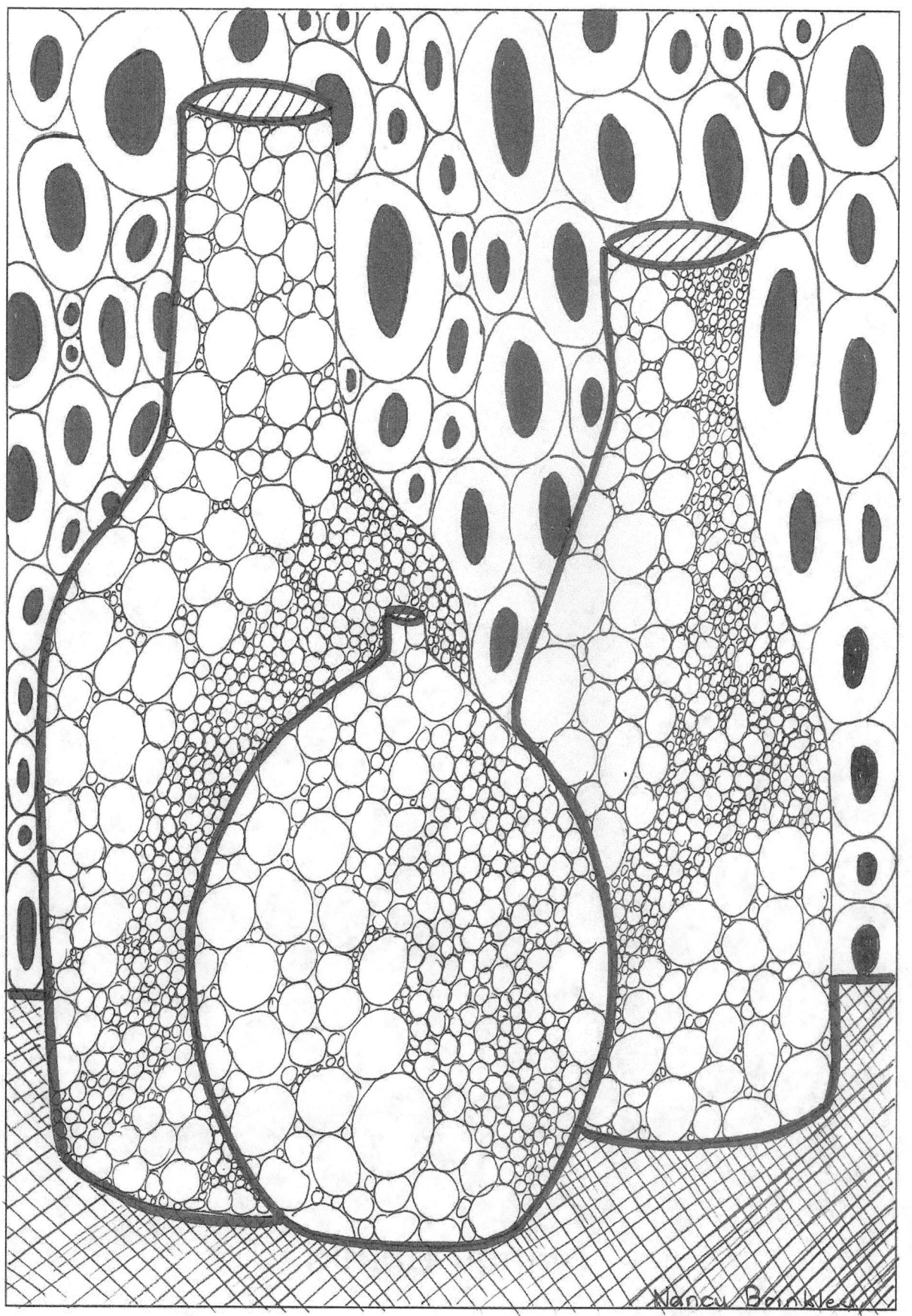

Nancy Brinkley

Nancy Brinkley

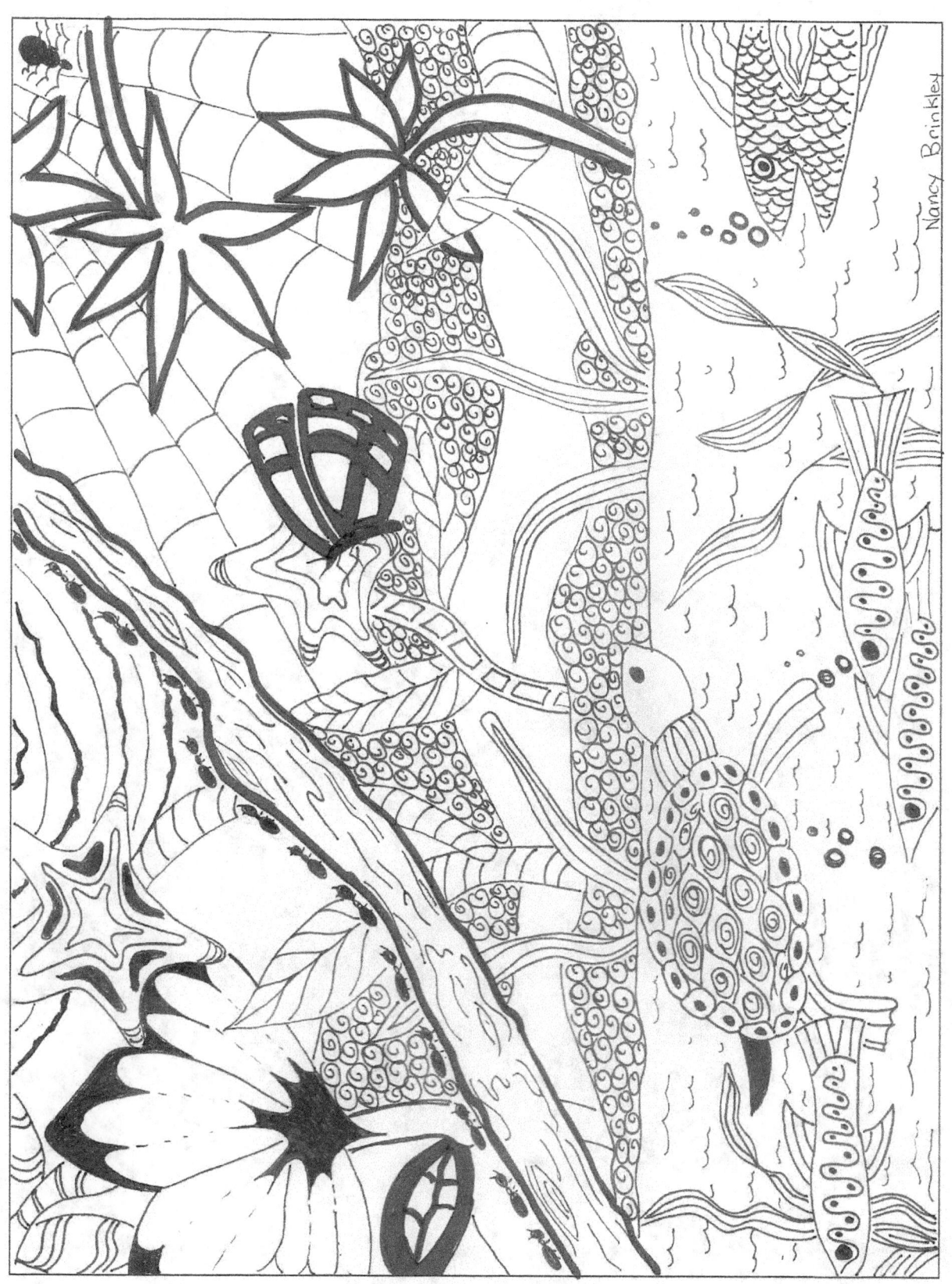

Nancy Brinkley

Nancy Brinkley

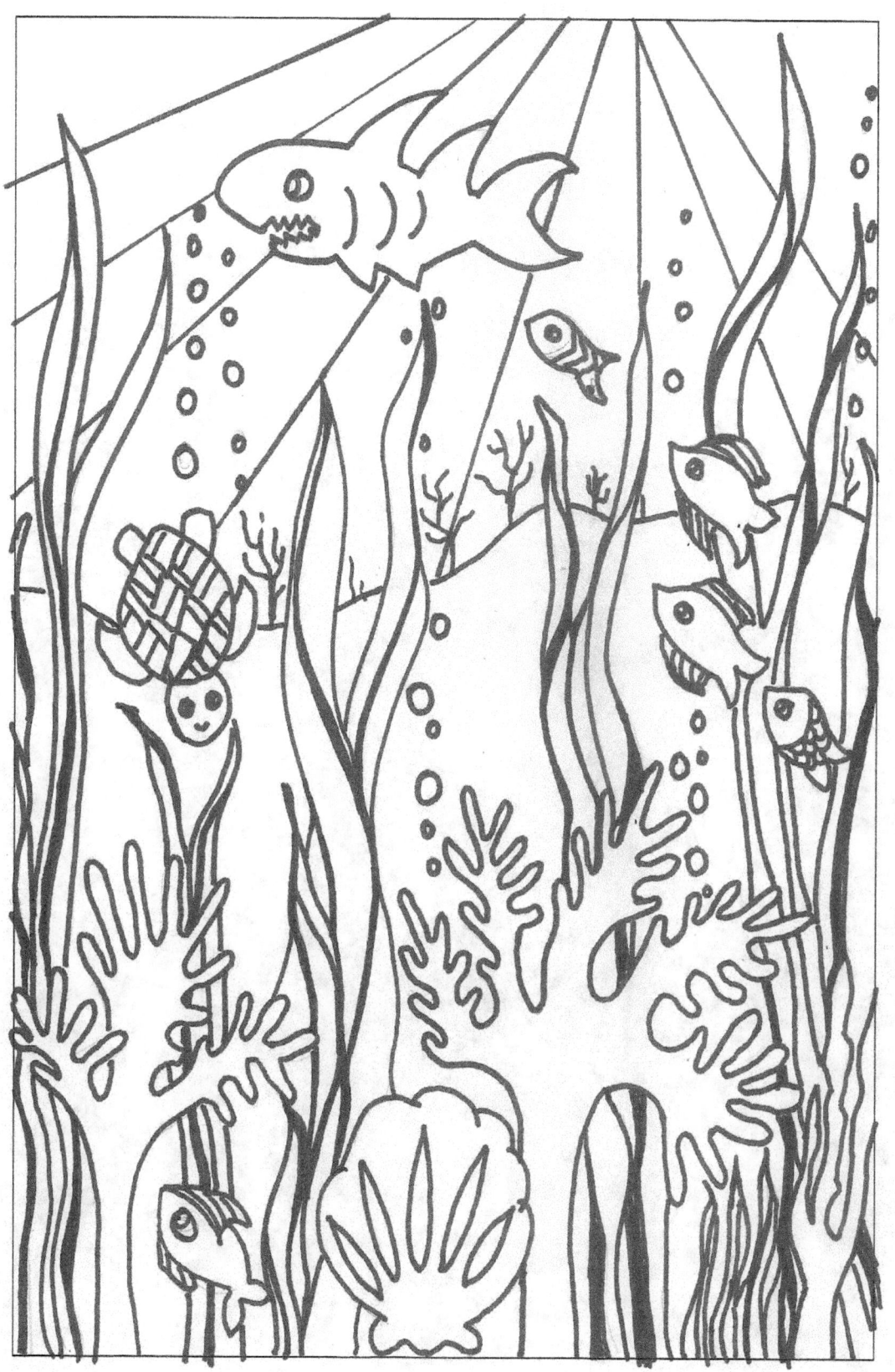

Dorothy Campbell

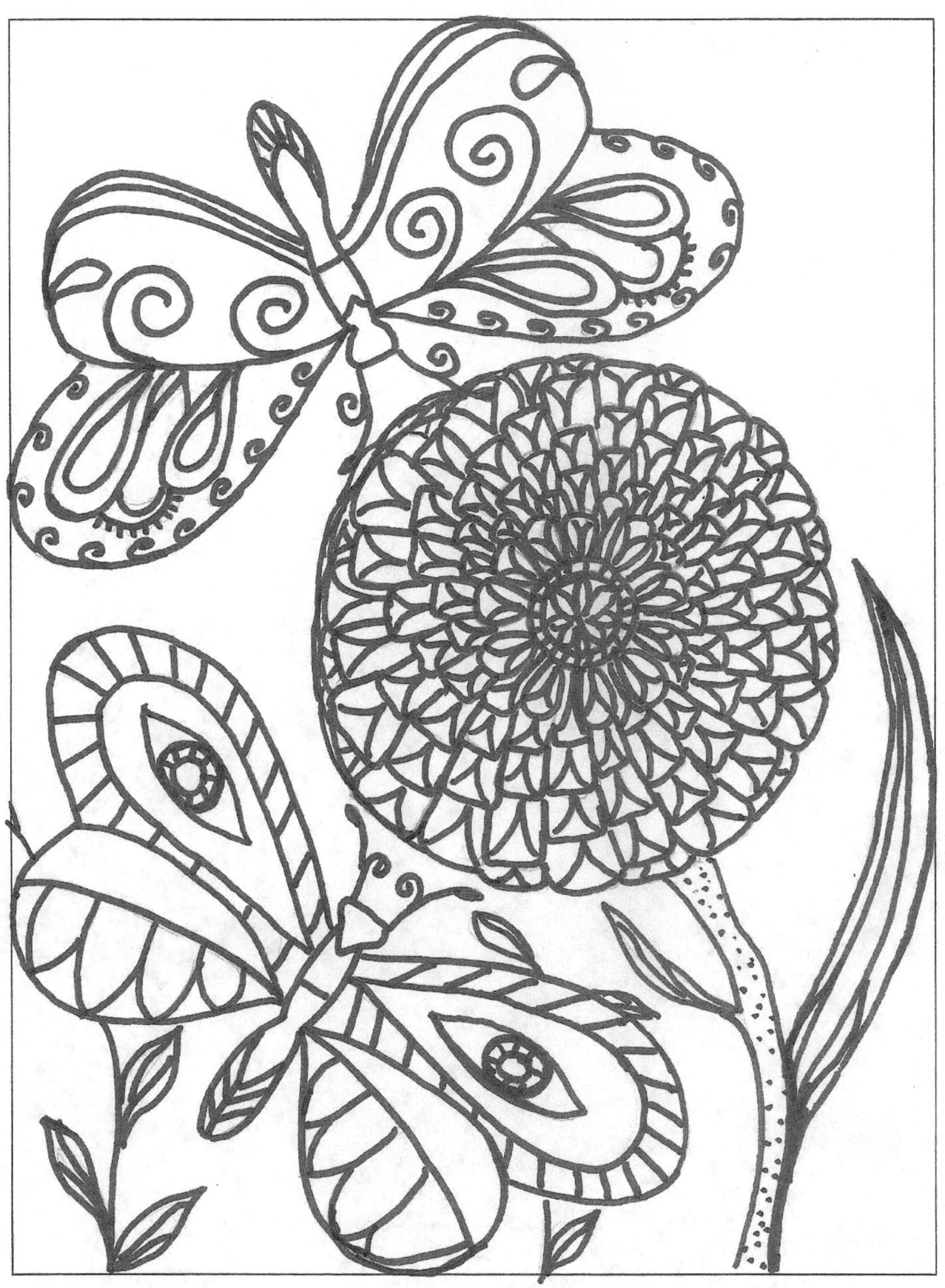

Dorothy Campbell

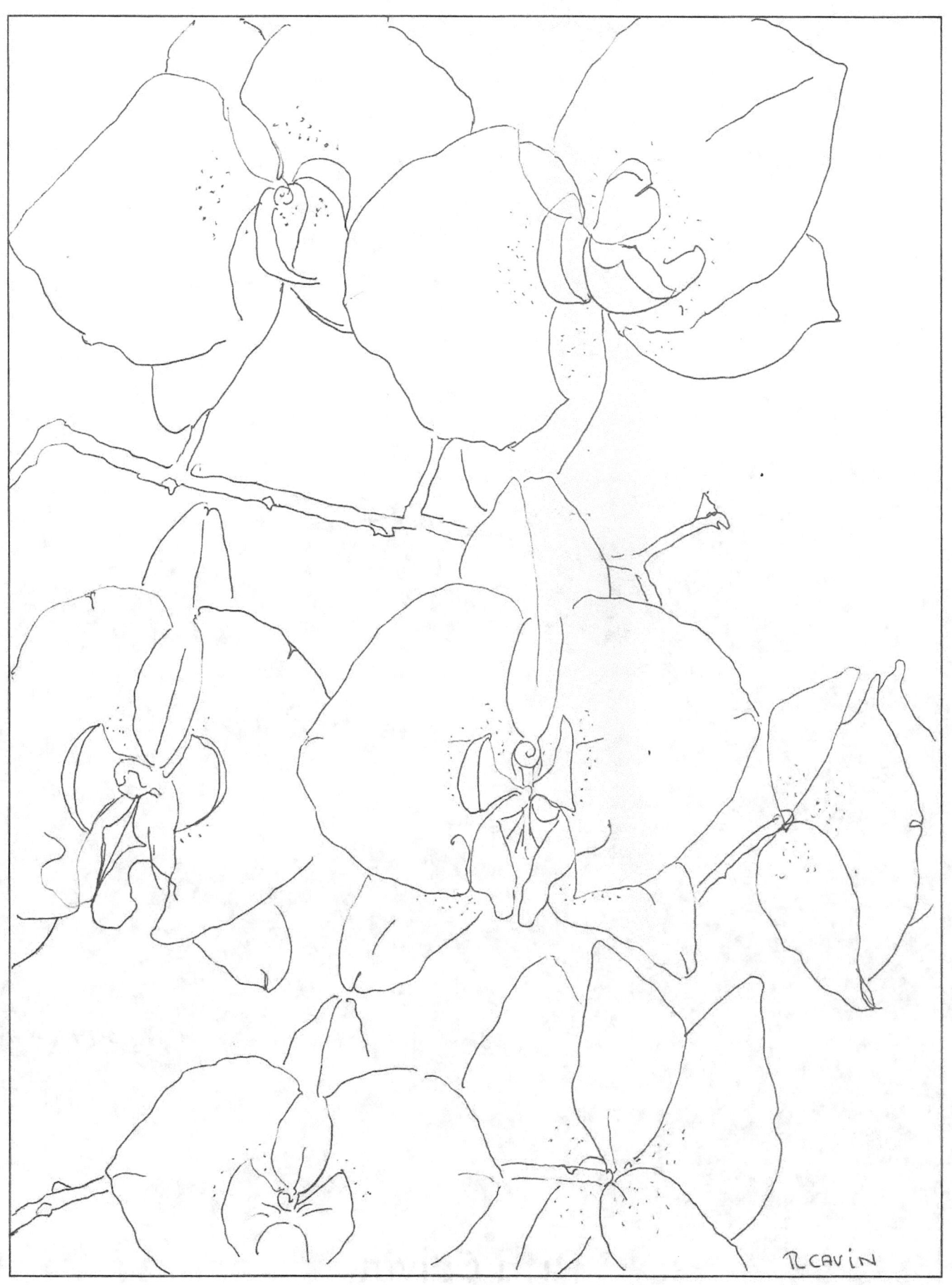

Rita Calvin

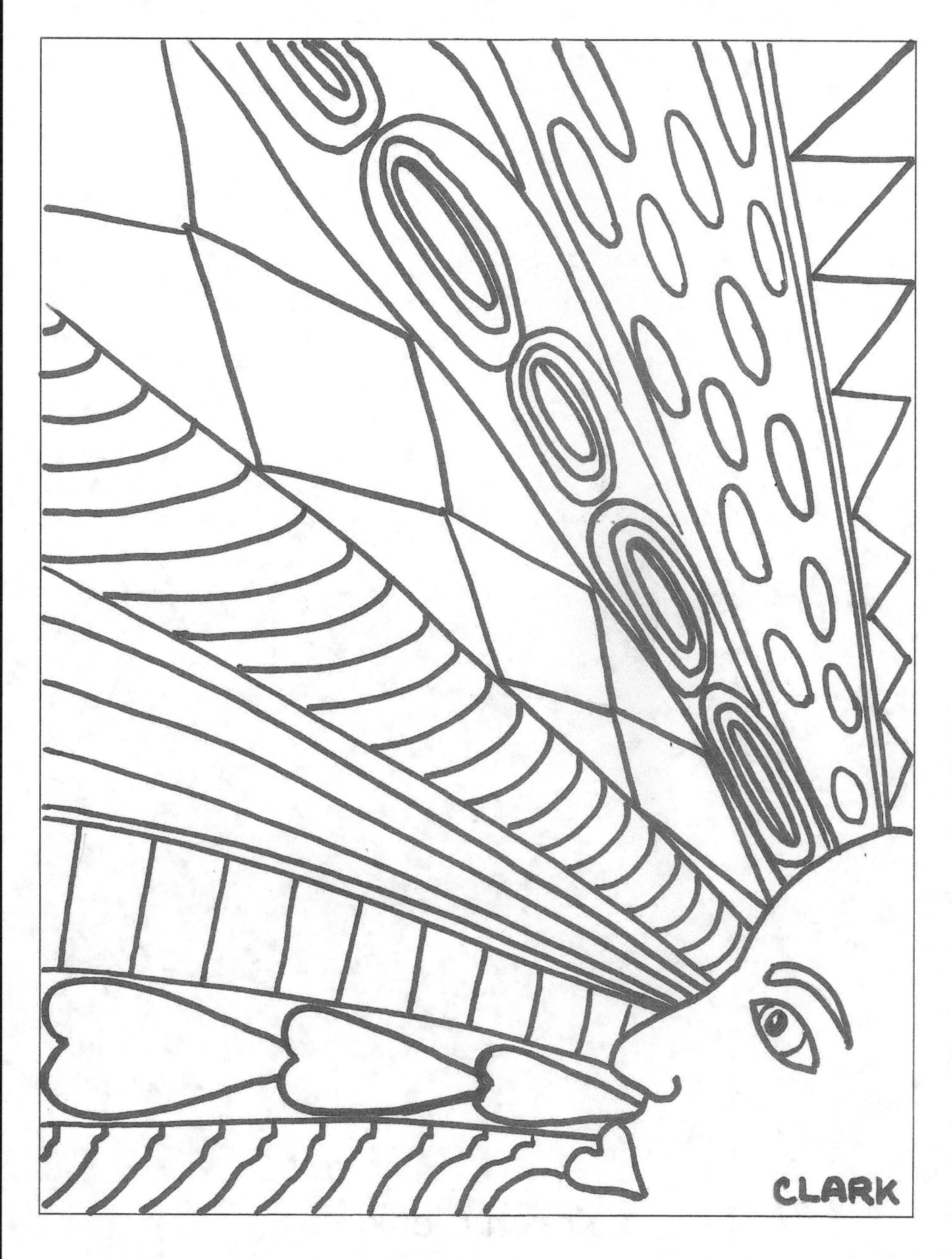

Karen Clark

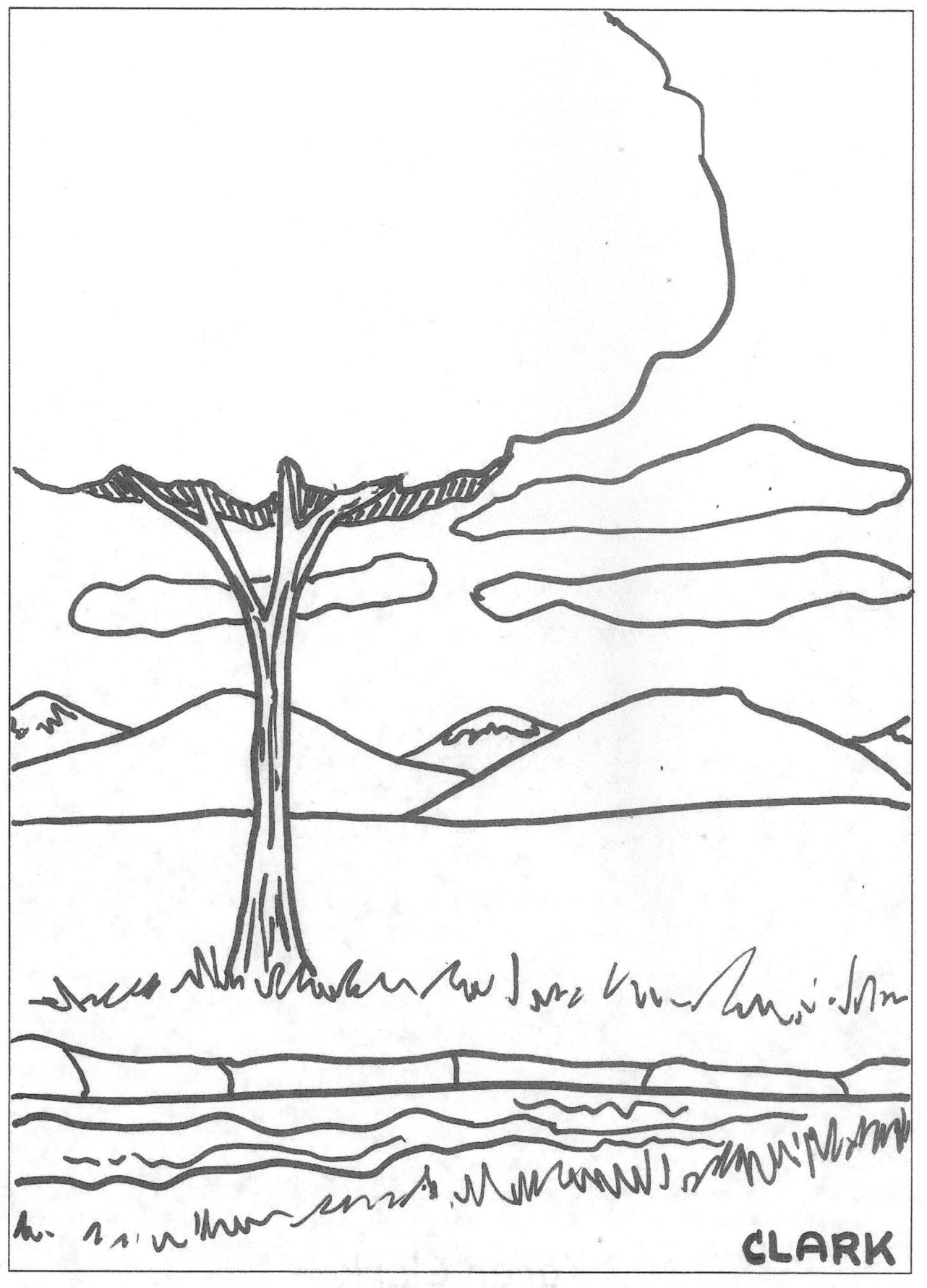

CLARK

Karen Clark

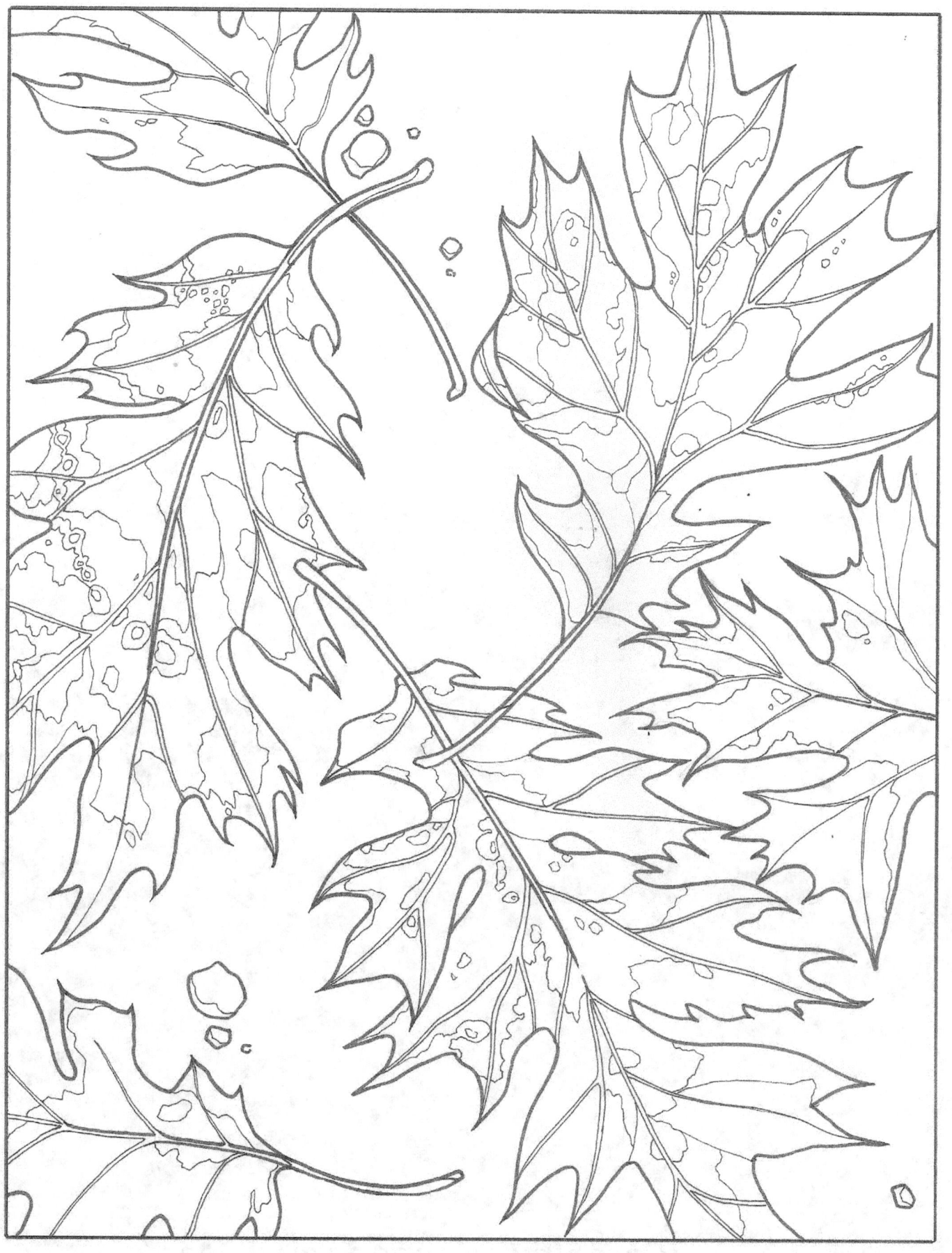

Carolyn Cunningham

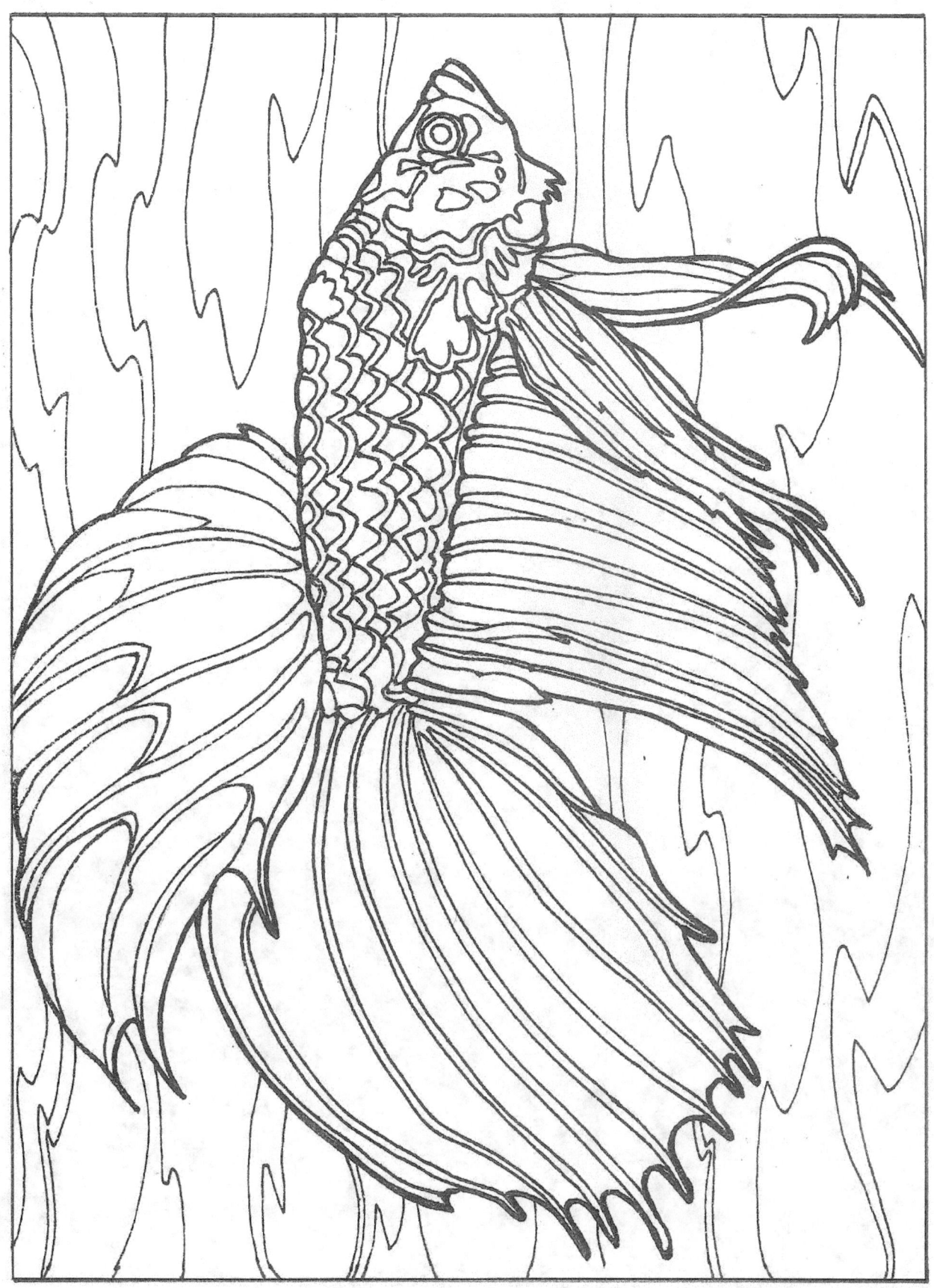

Carolyn Cunningham

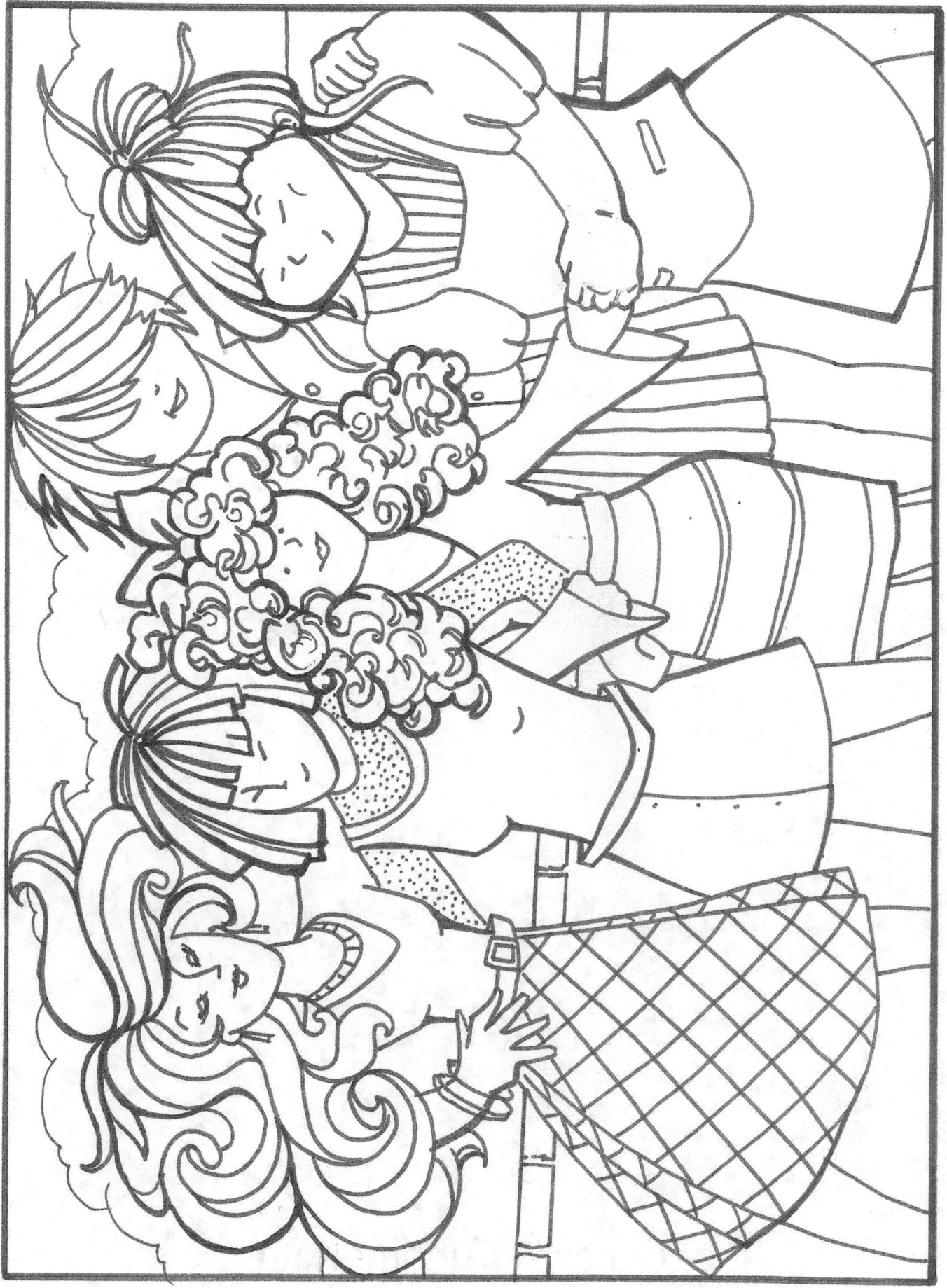

Carolyn Cunningham

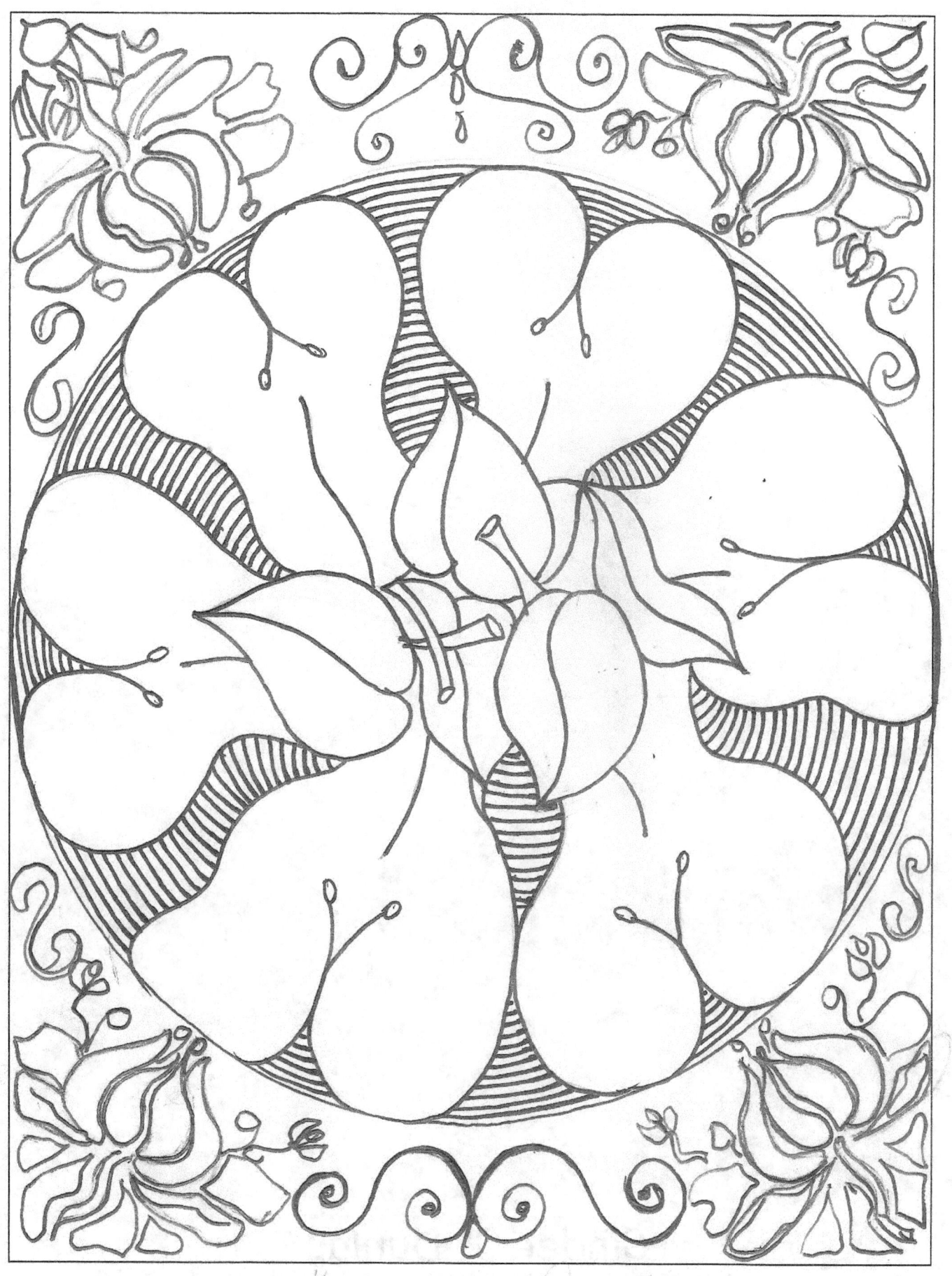

" Kandinsky Pears "

Cindee J. Dunlap

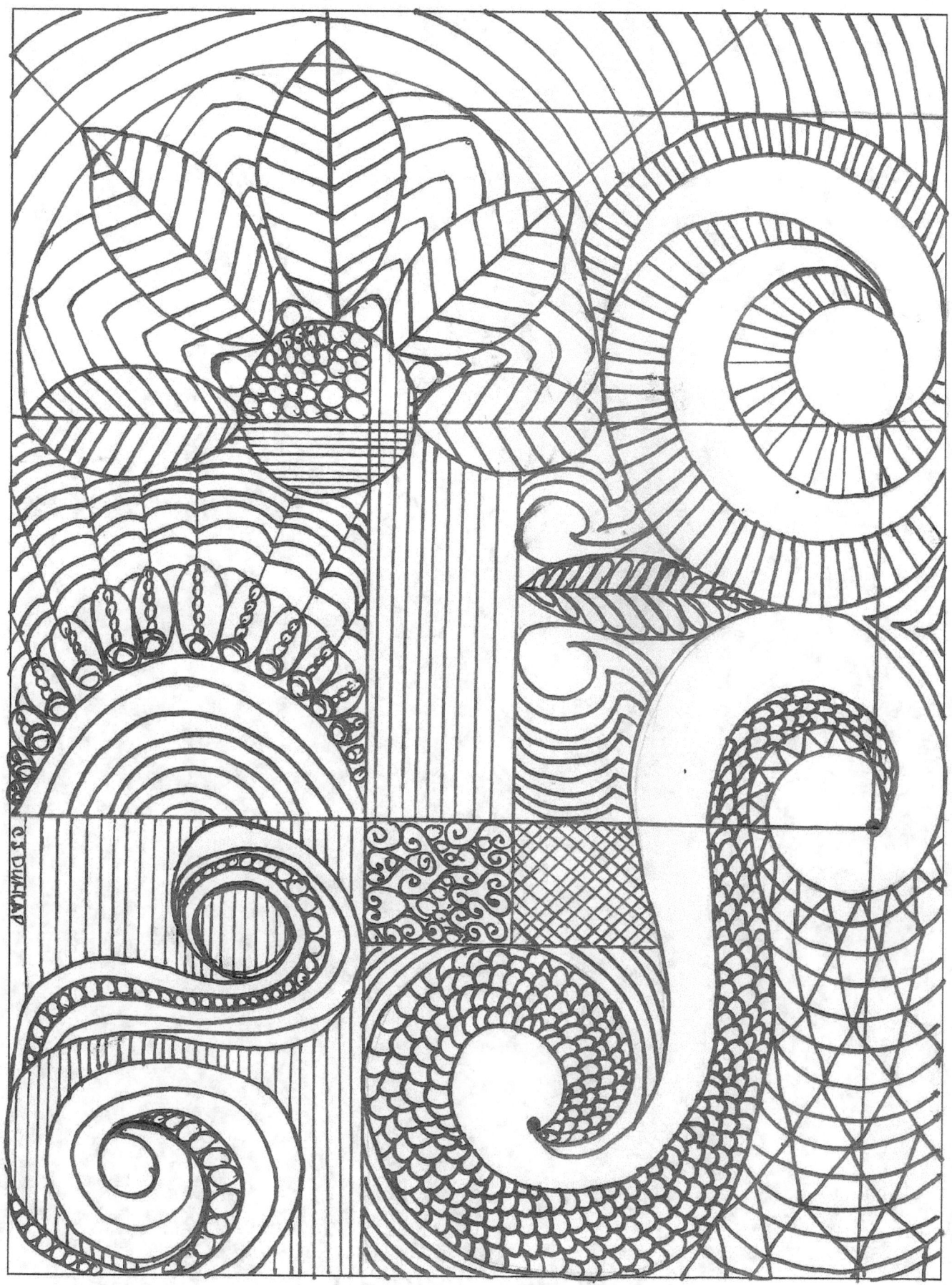

Cindee J. Dunlap

Lynn Fearman

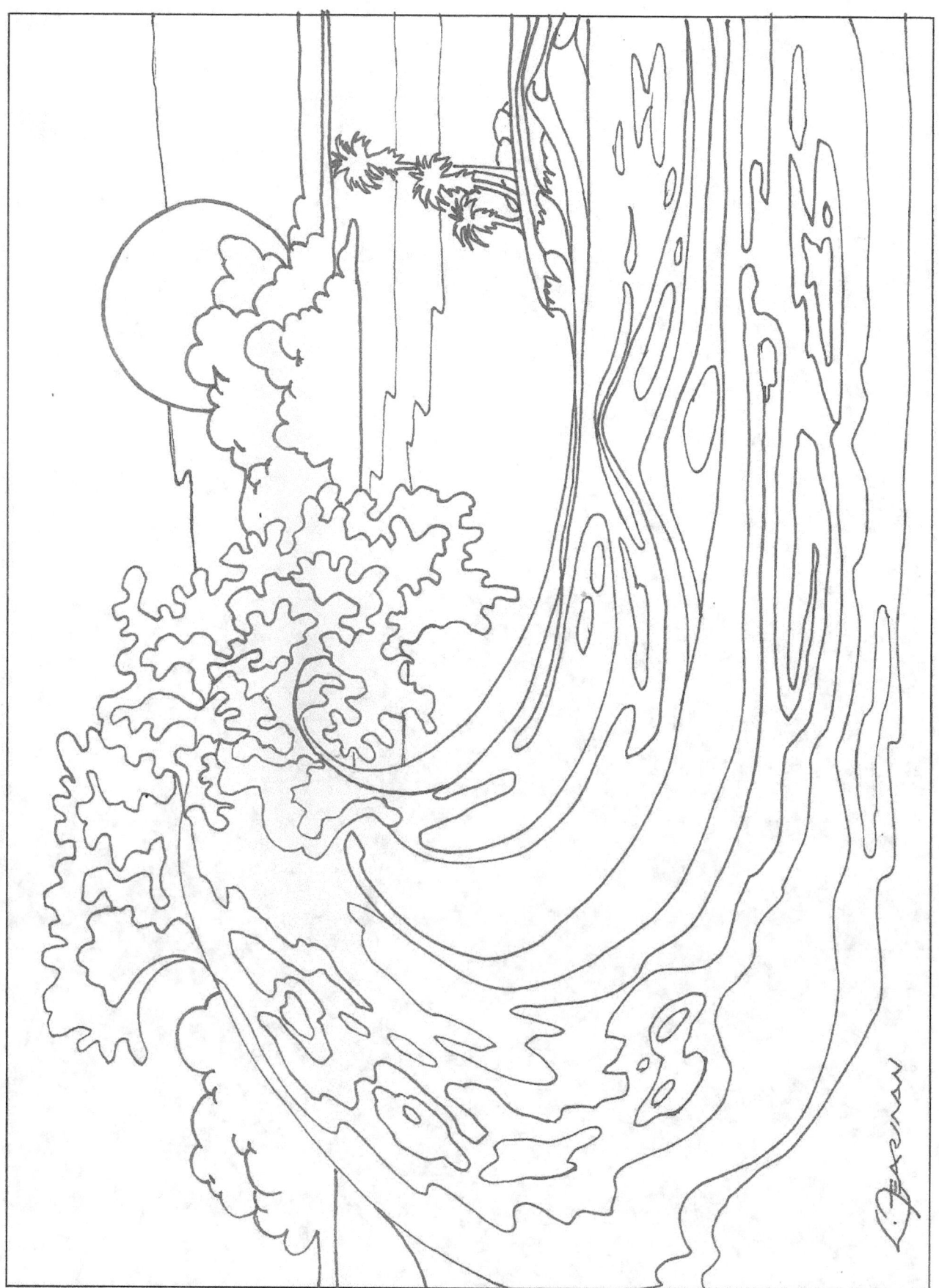

Lynn Fearman

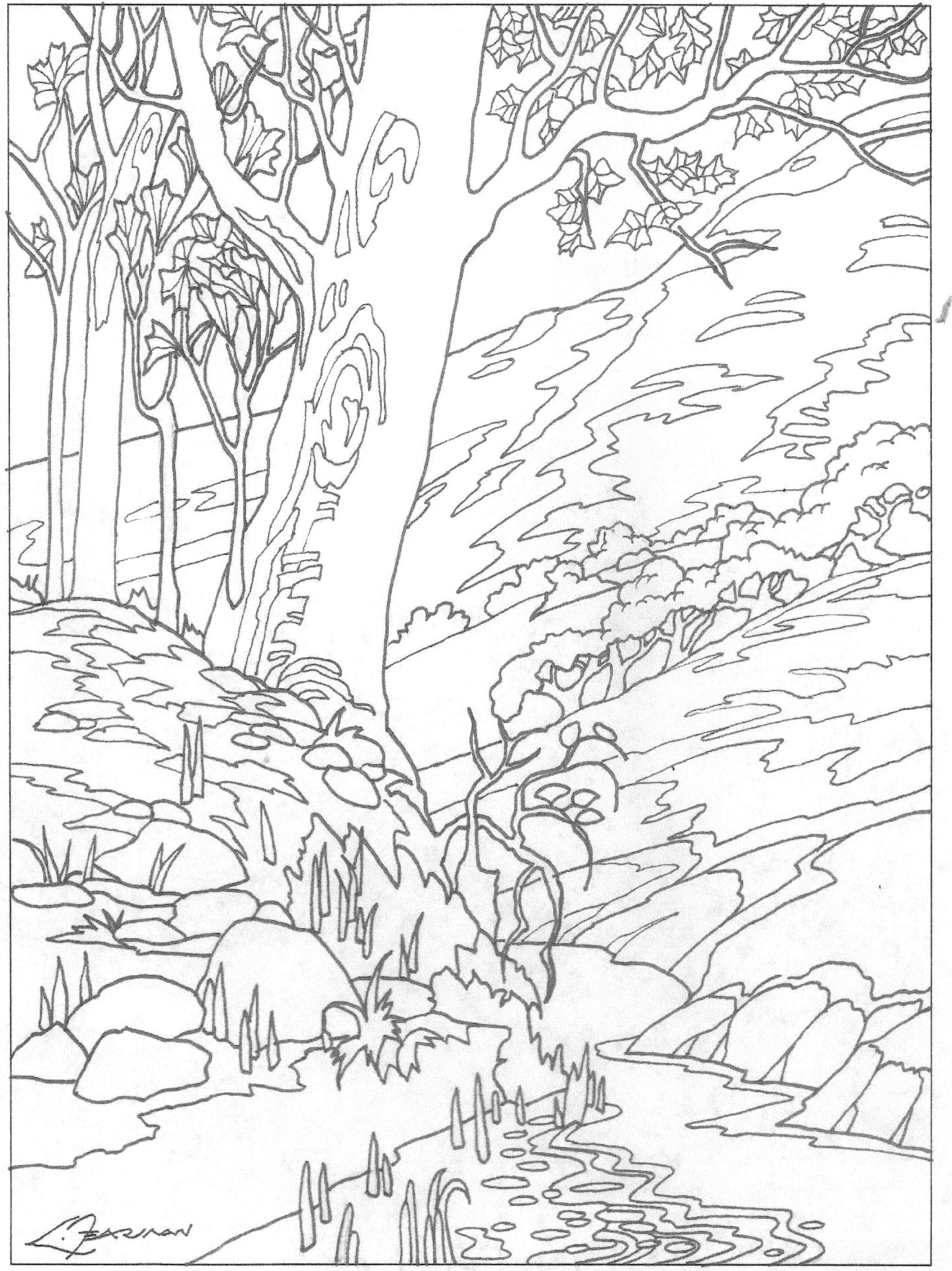

Lynn Fearman

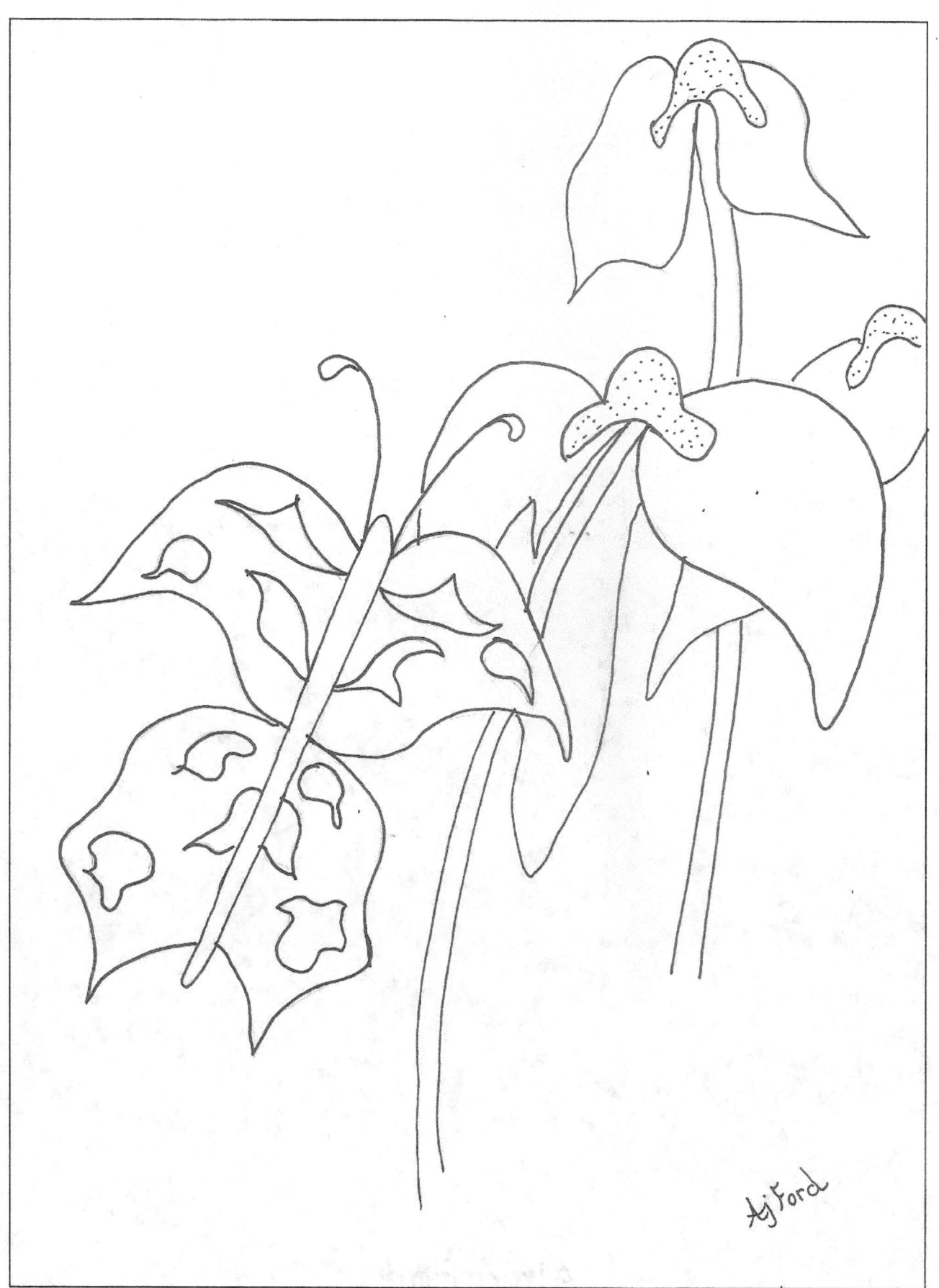

AjFord

Alma Ford

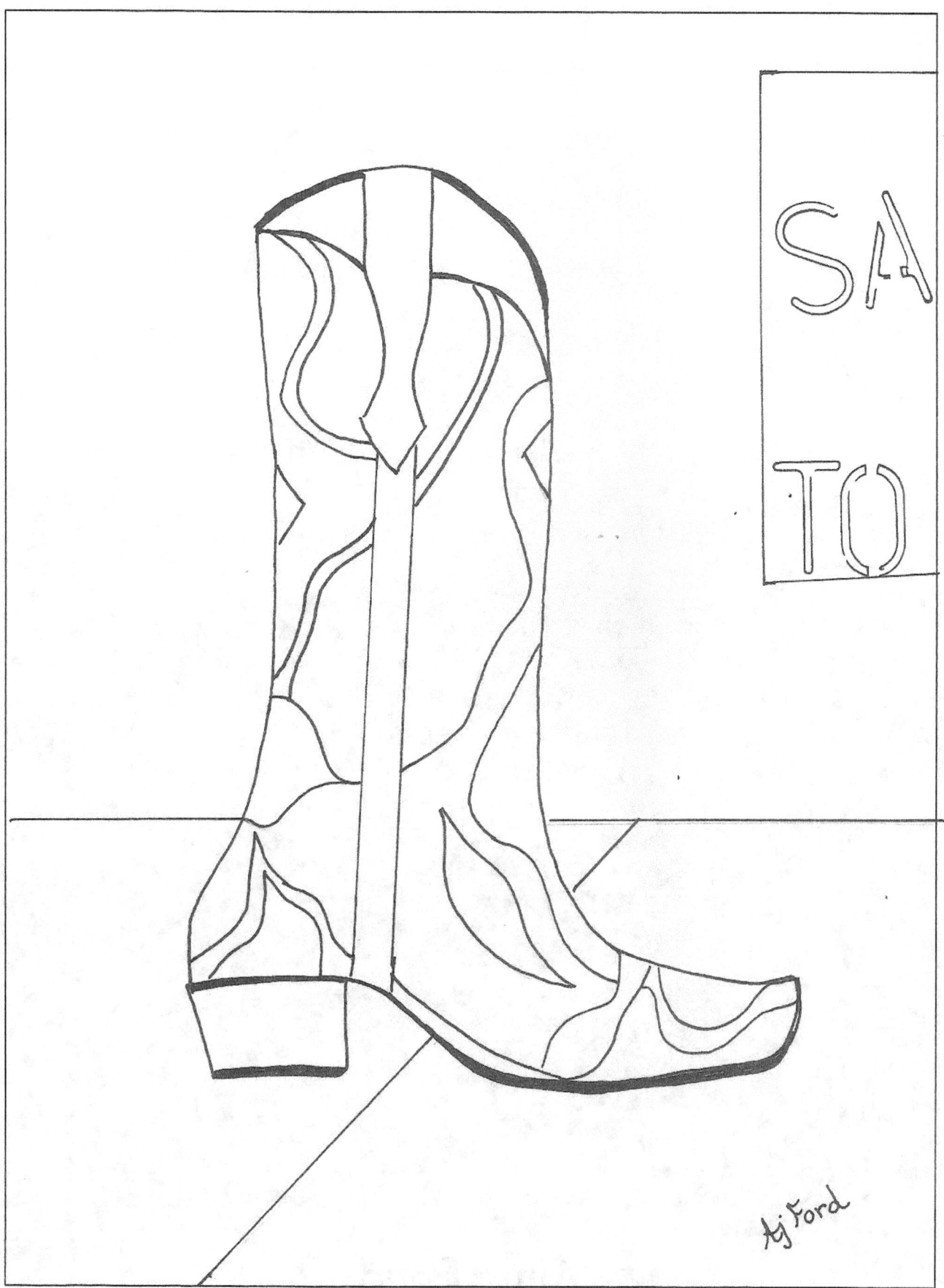

SA

TO

Aj Ford

Alma Ford

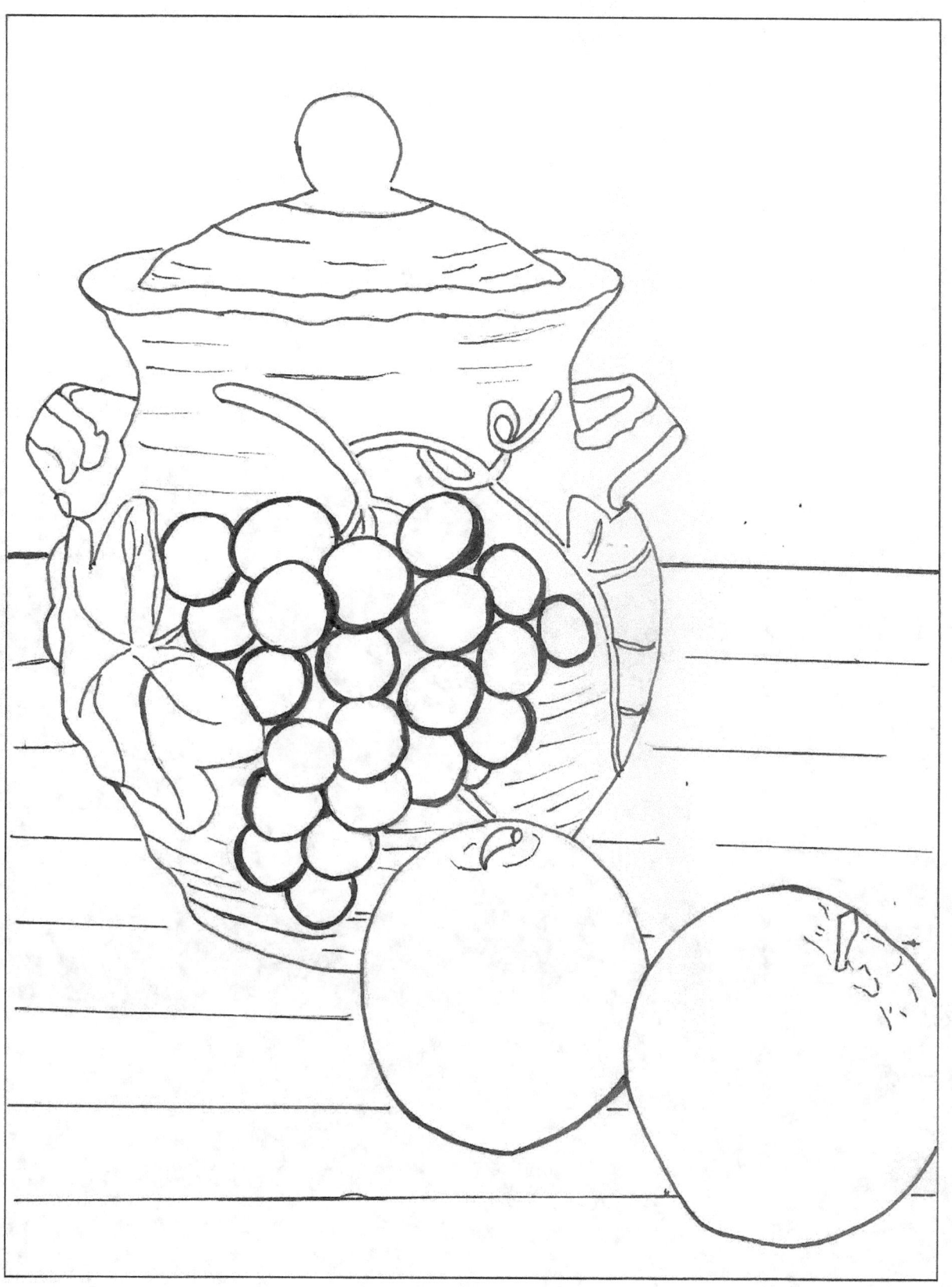

Sandi Grimley

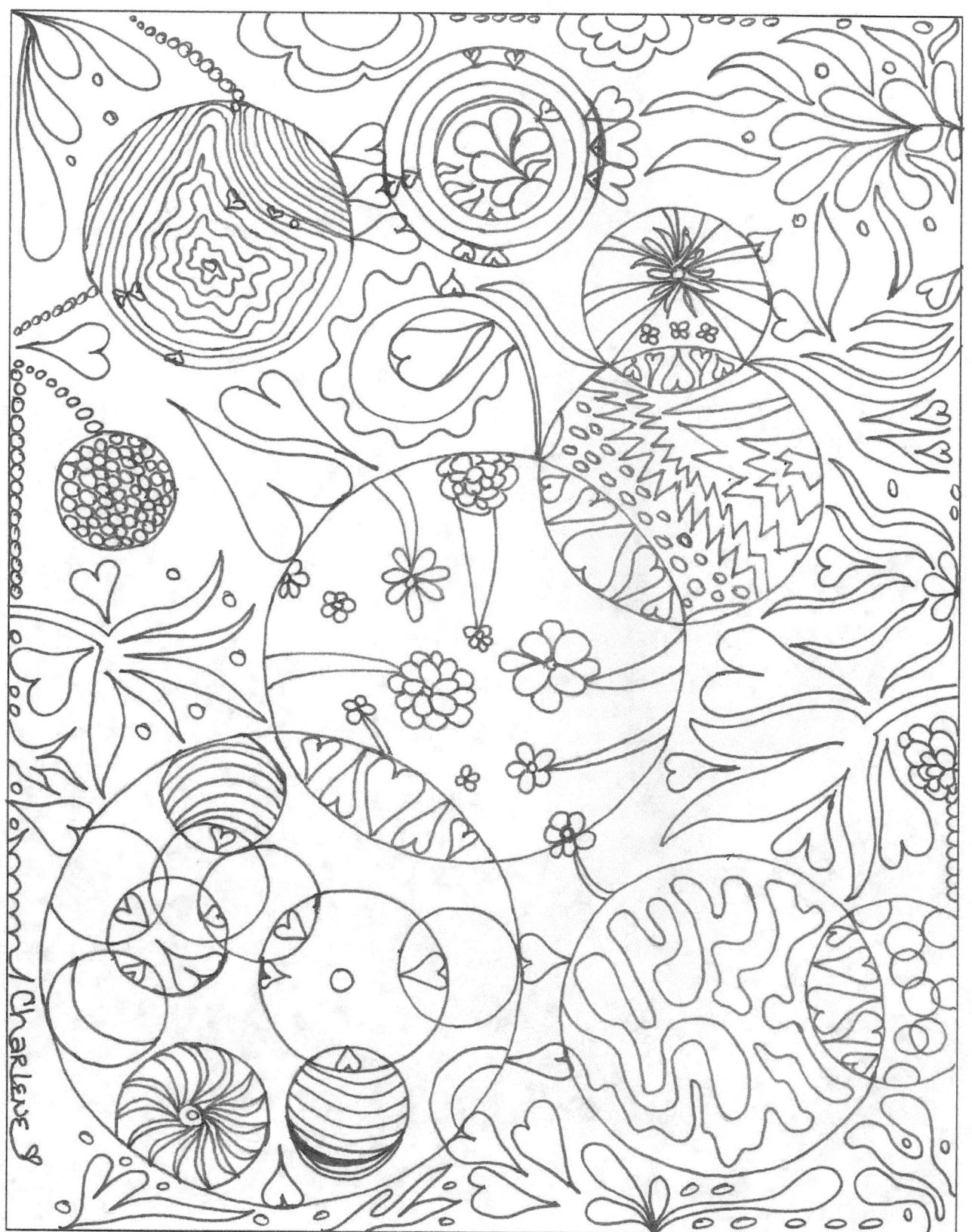

Charlene Hobbs

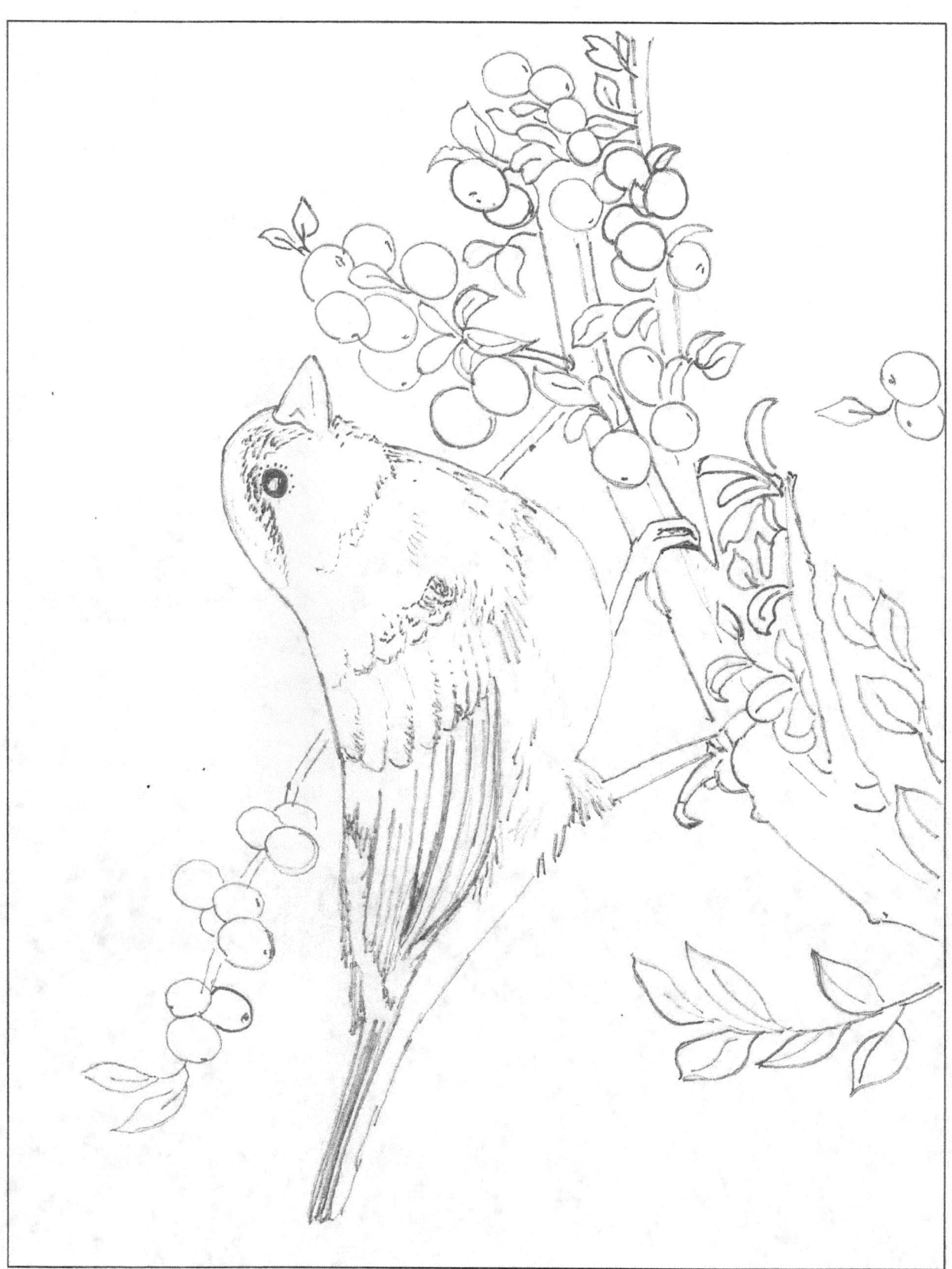

Jan Hydeman

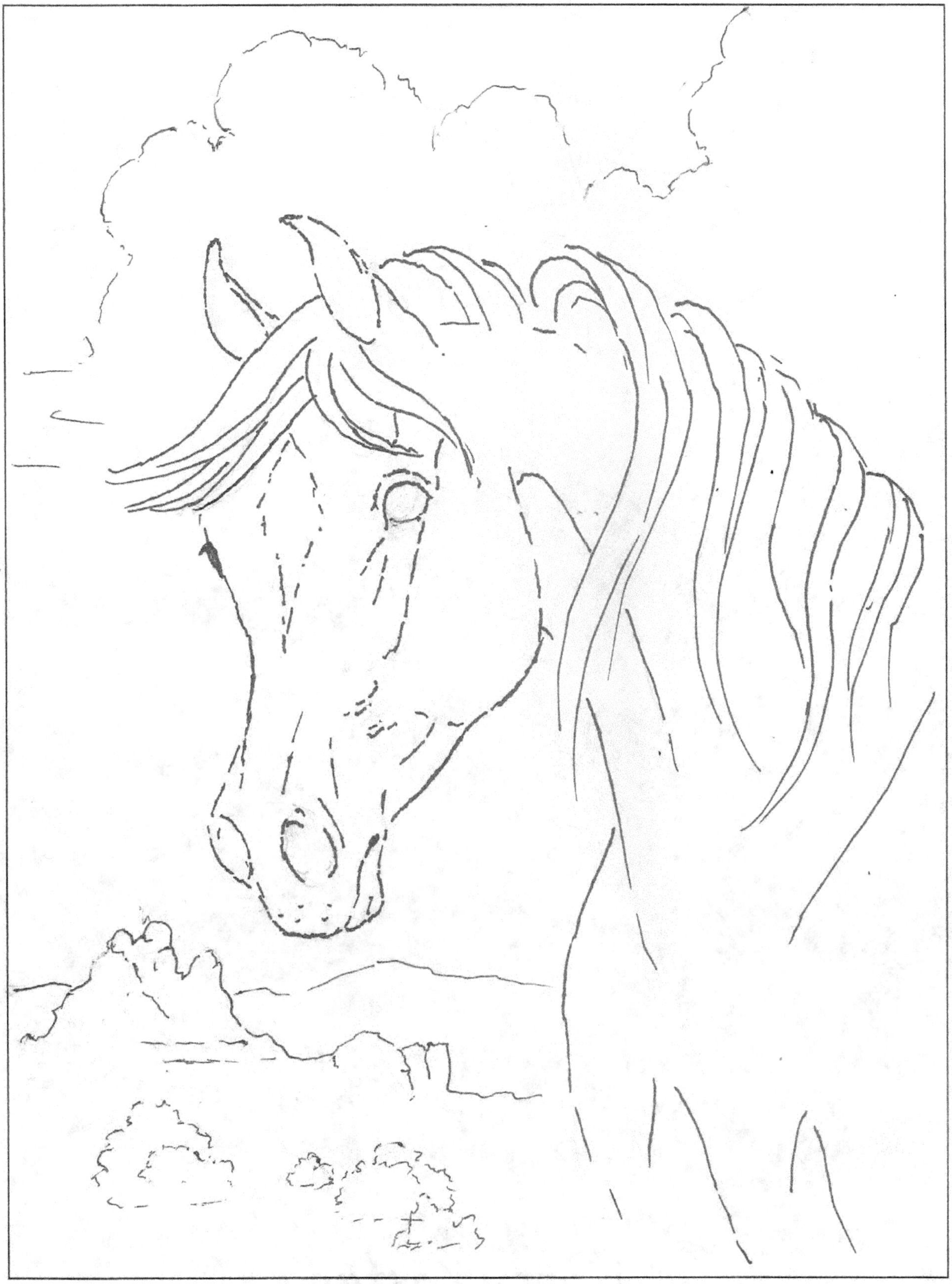

Nancy Kasten

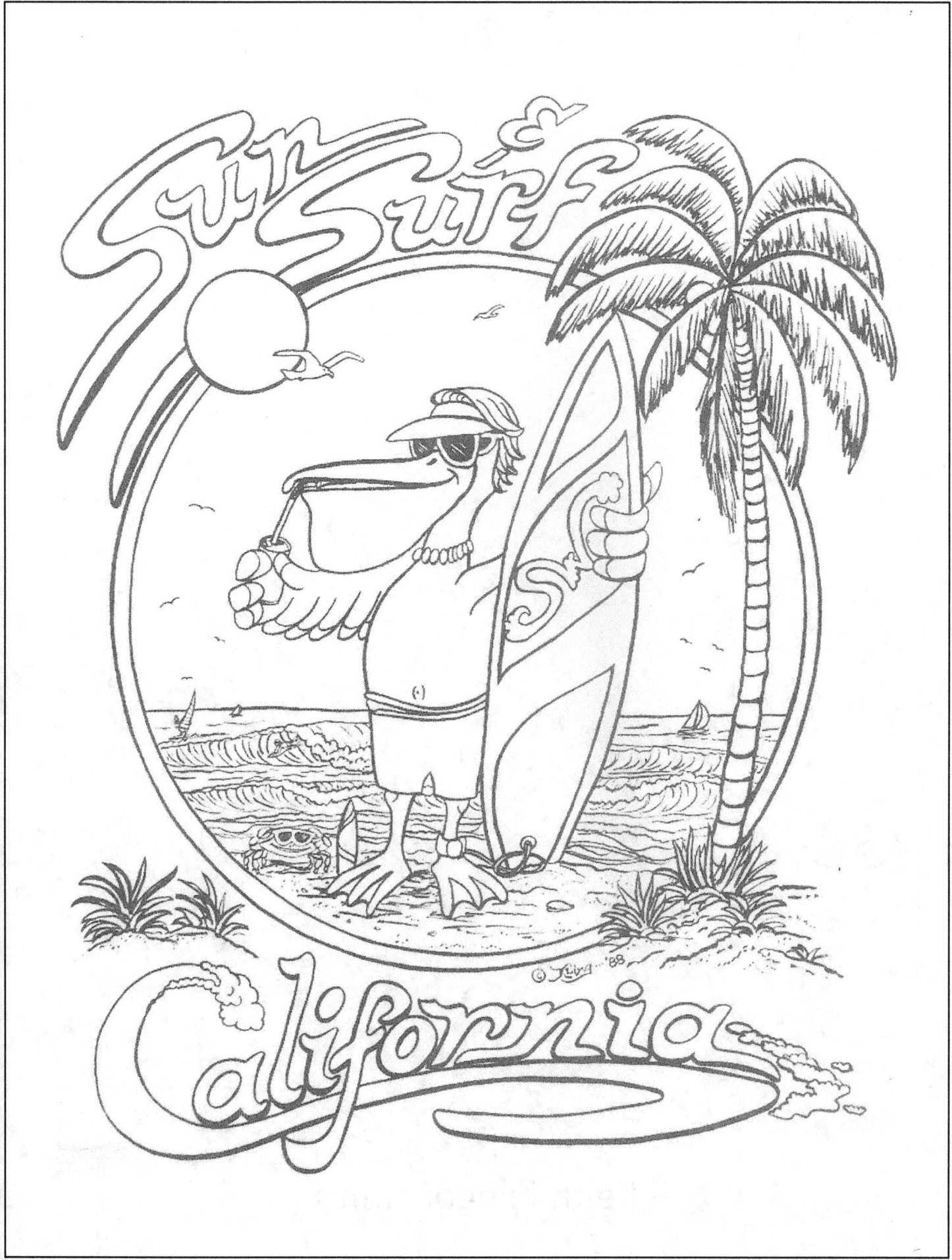

Keith Klingonsmith

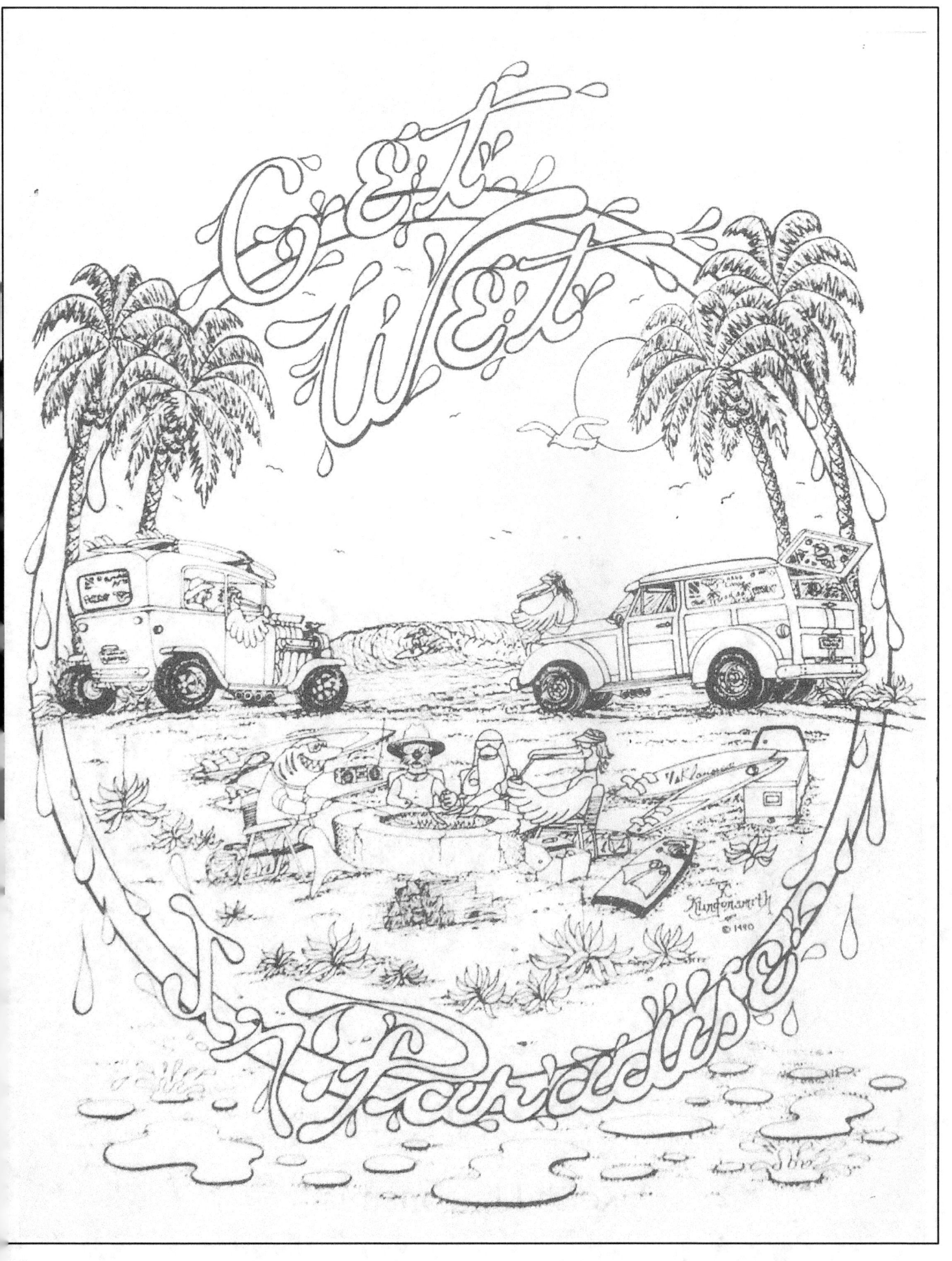

Keith Klingonsmit

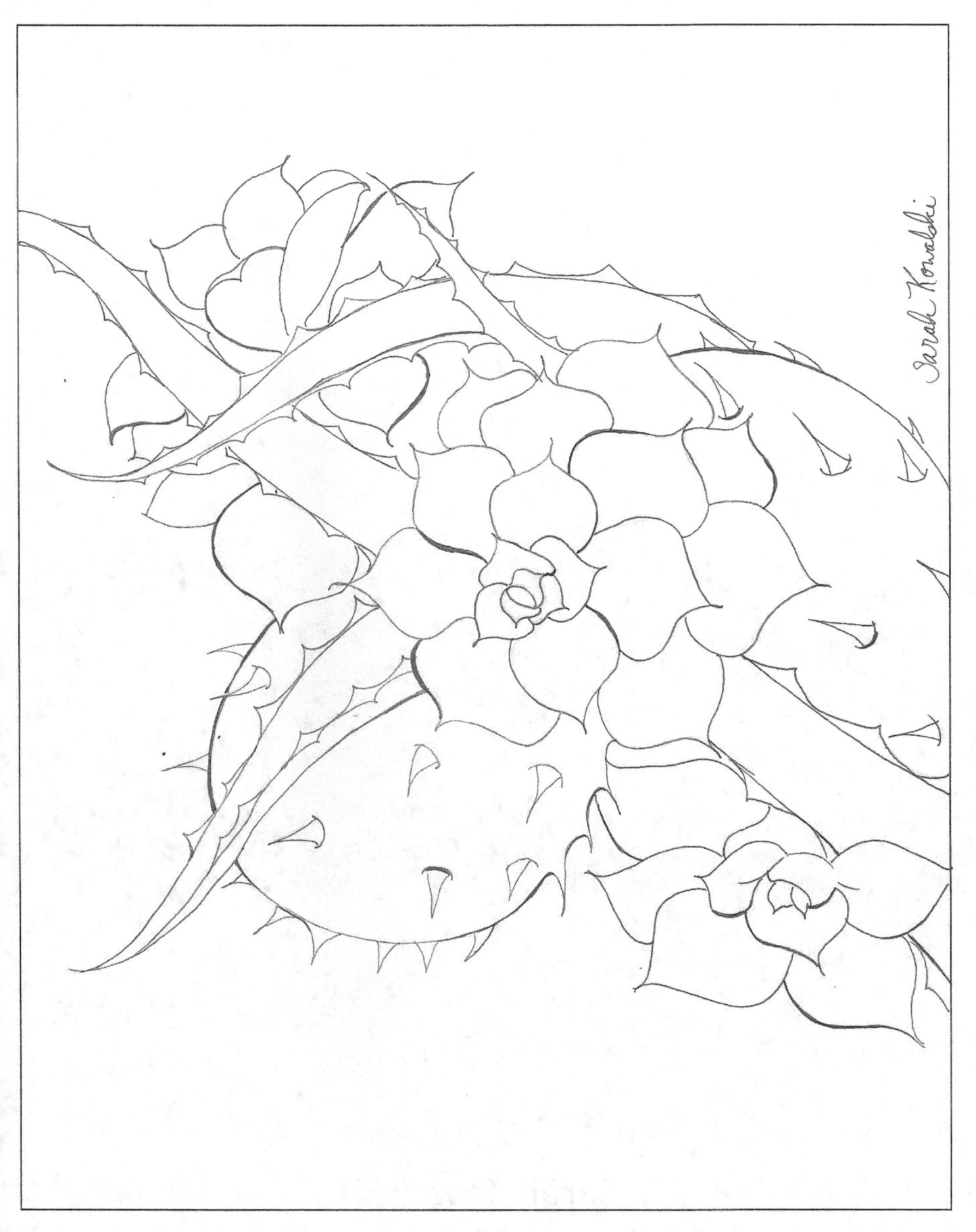

Sarah Konoski

Sarah Kowalski

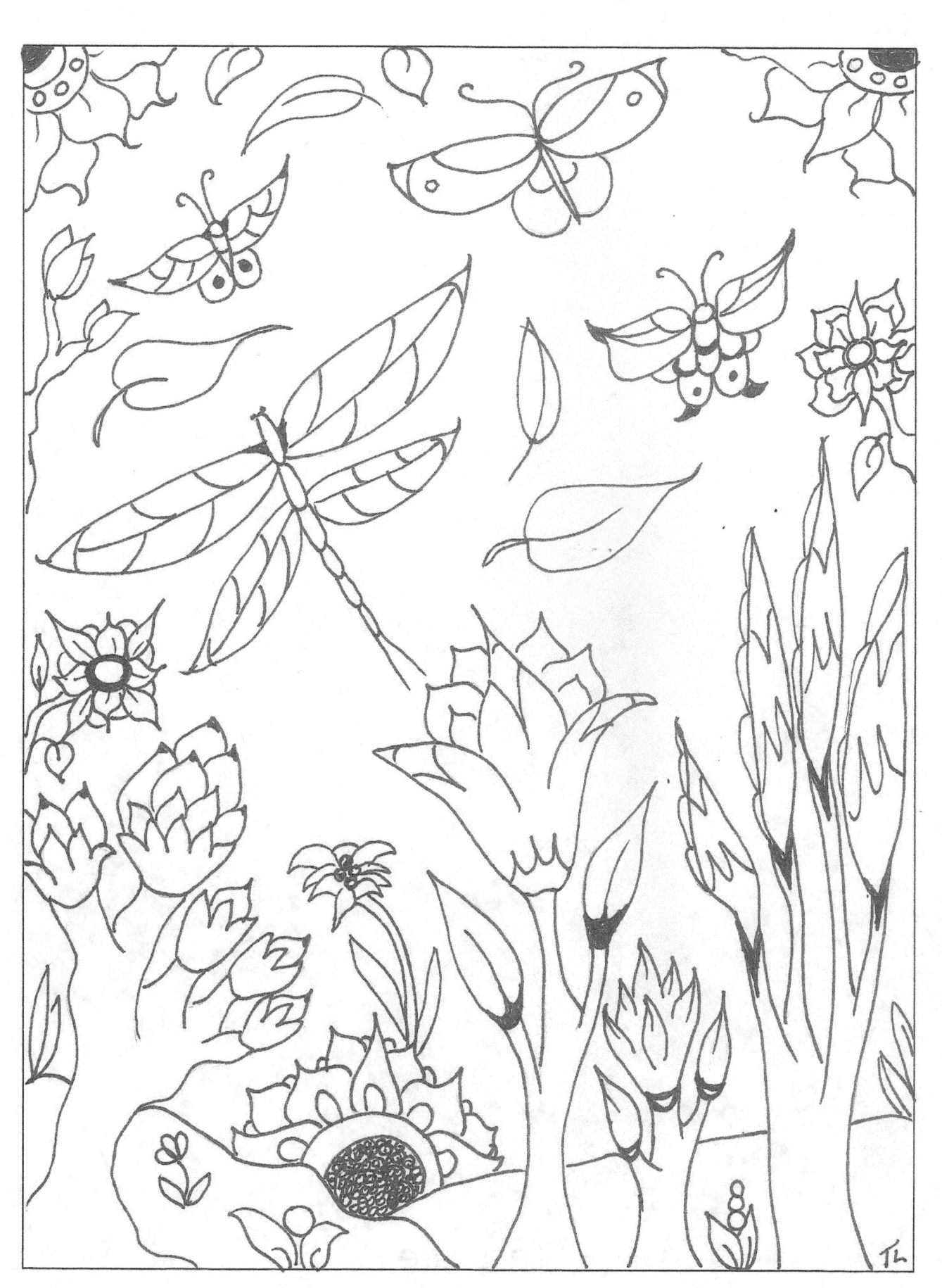

Tess Lee

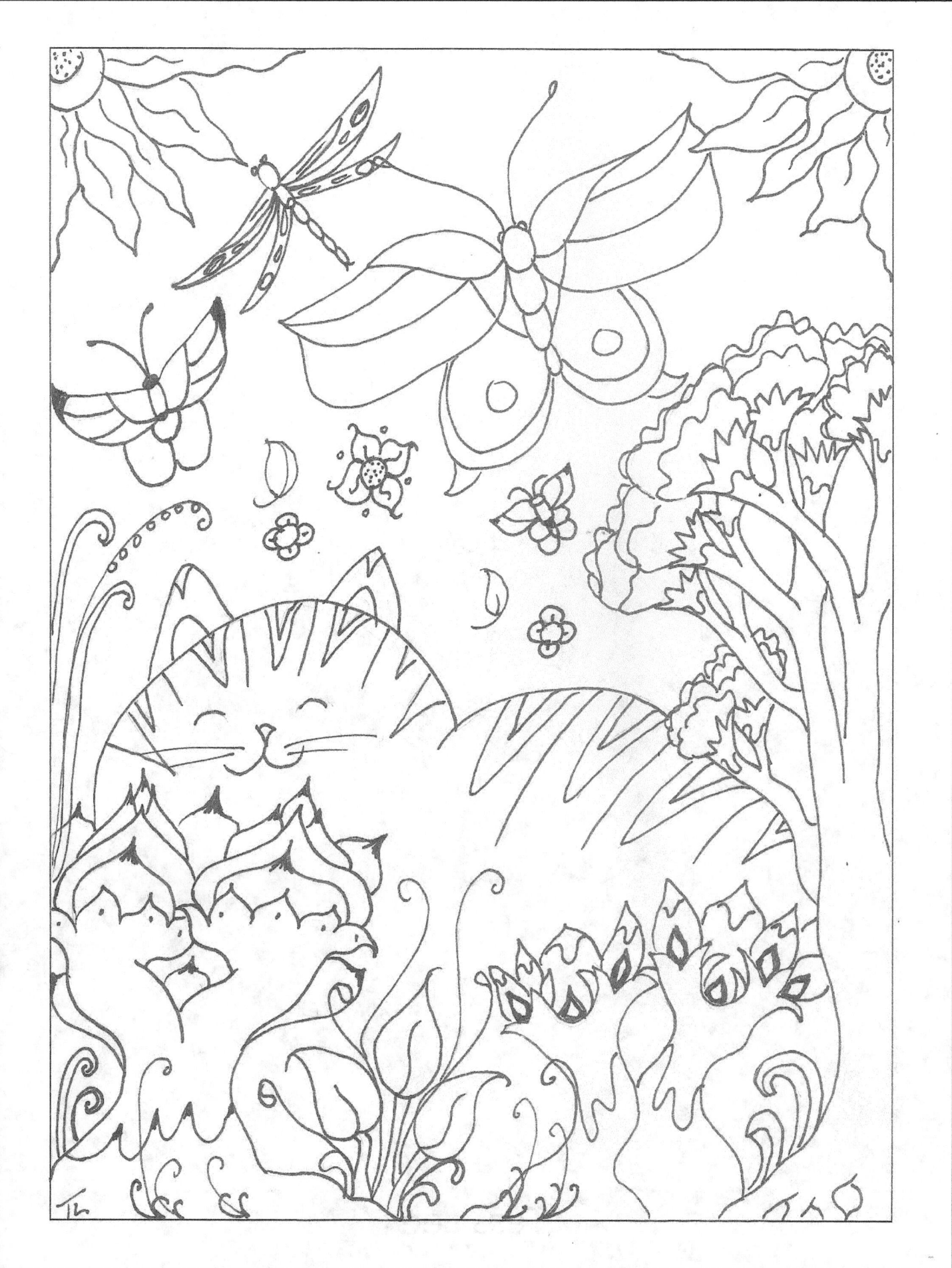

Tess Lee

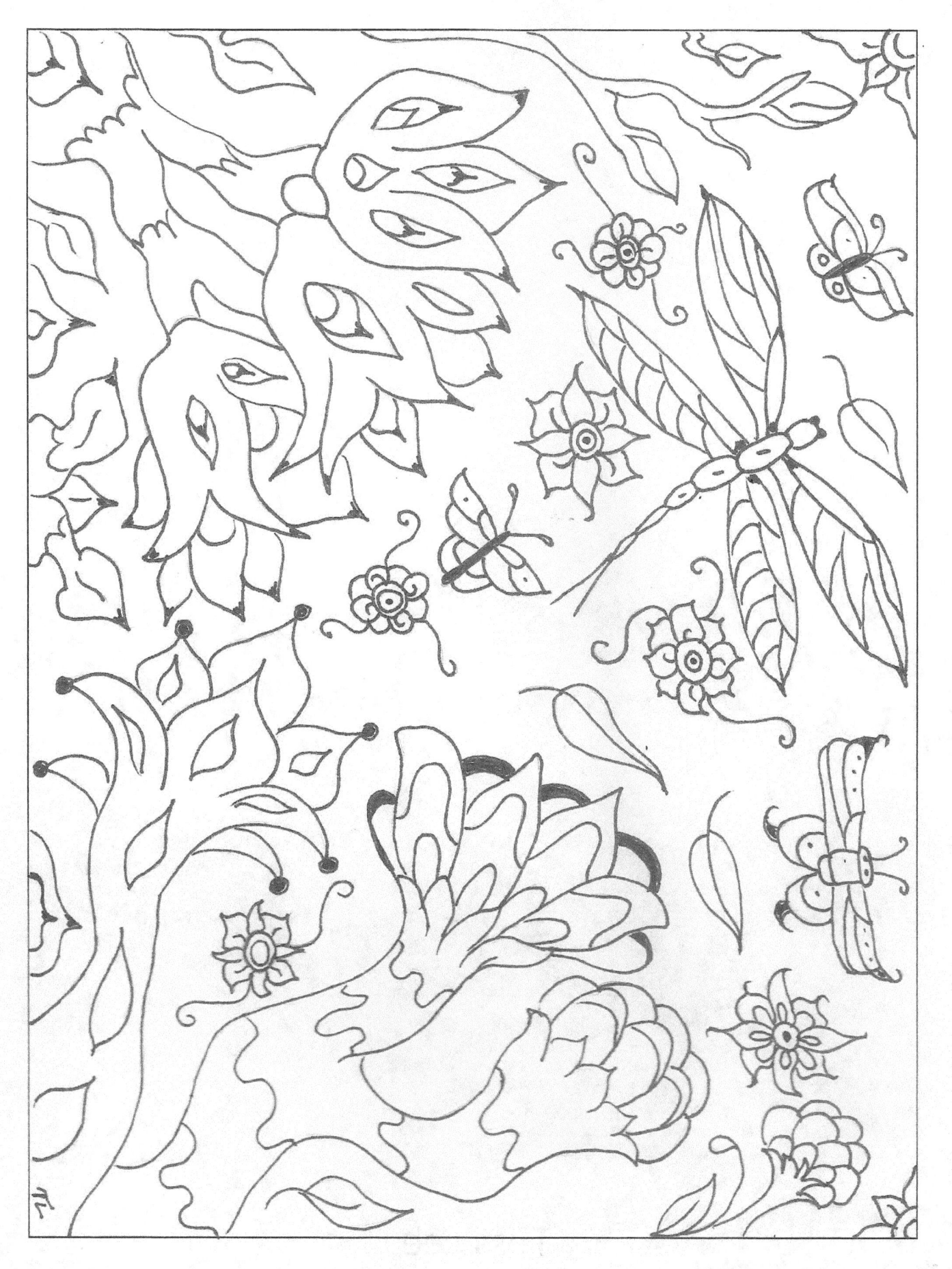

Tess Lee

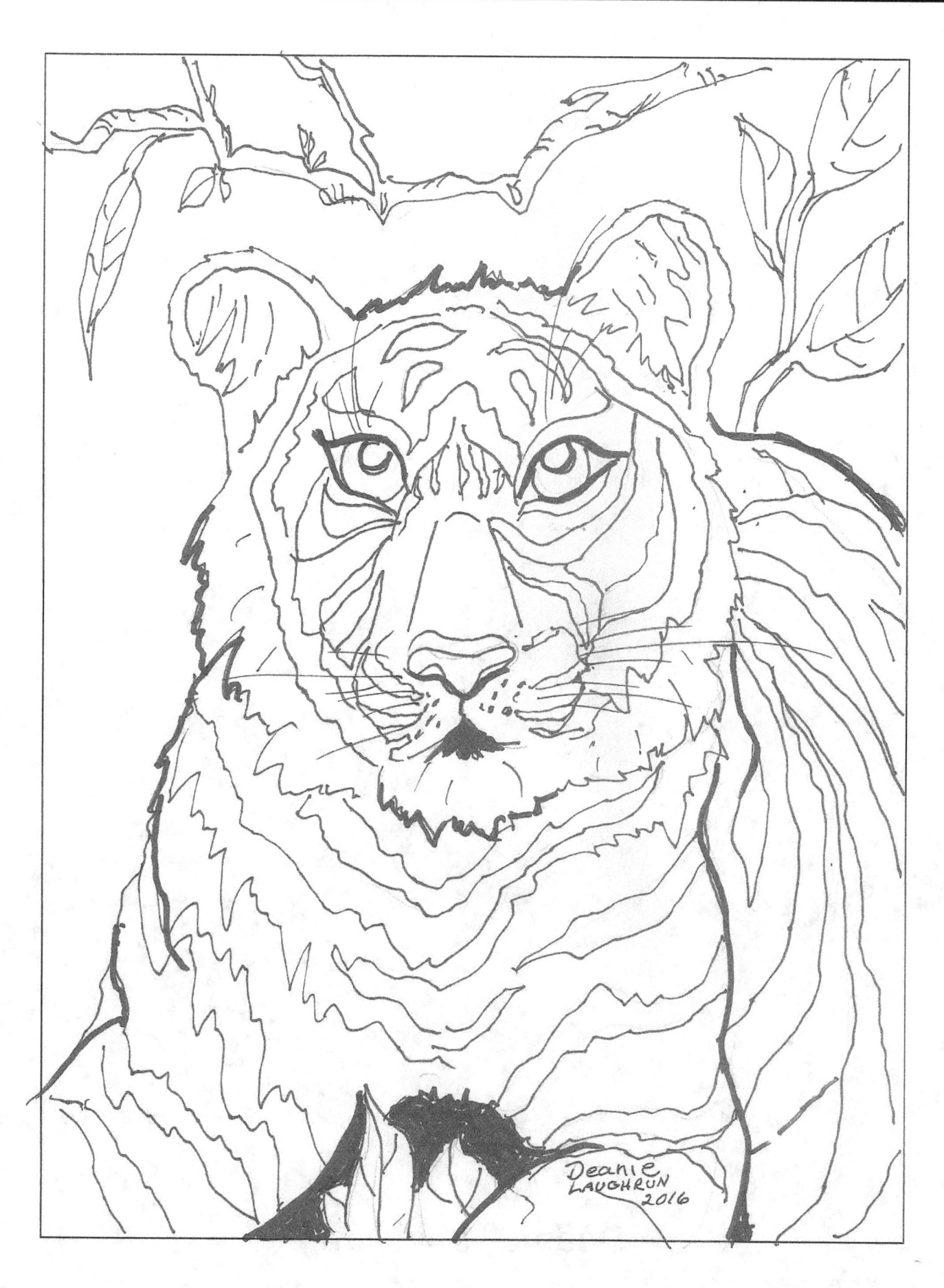

Deanie
Laughrun
2016

Deanie Laughrun

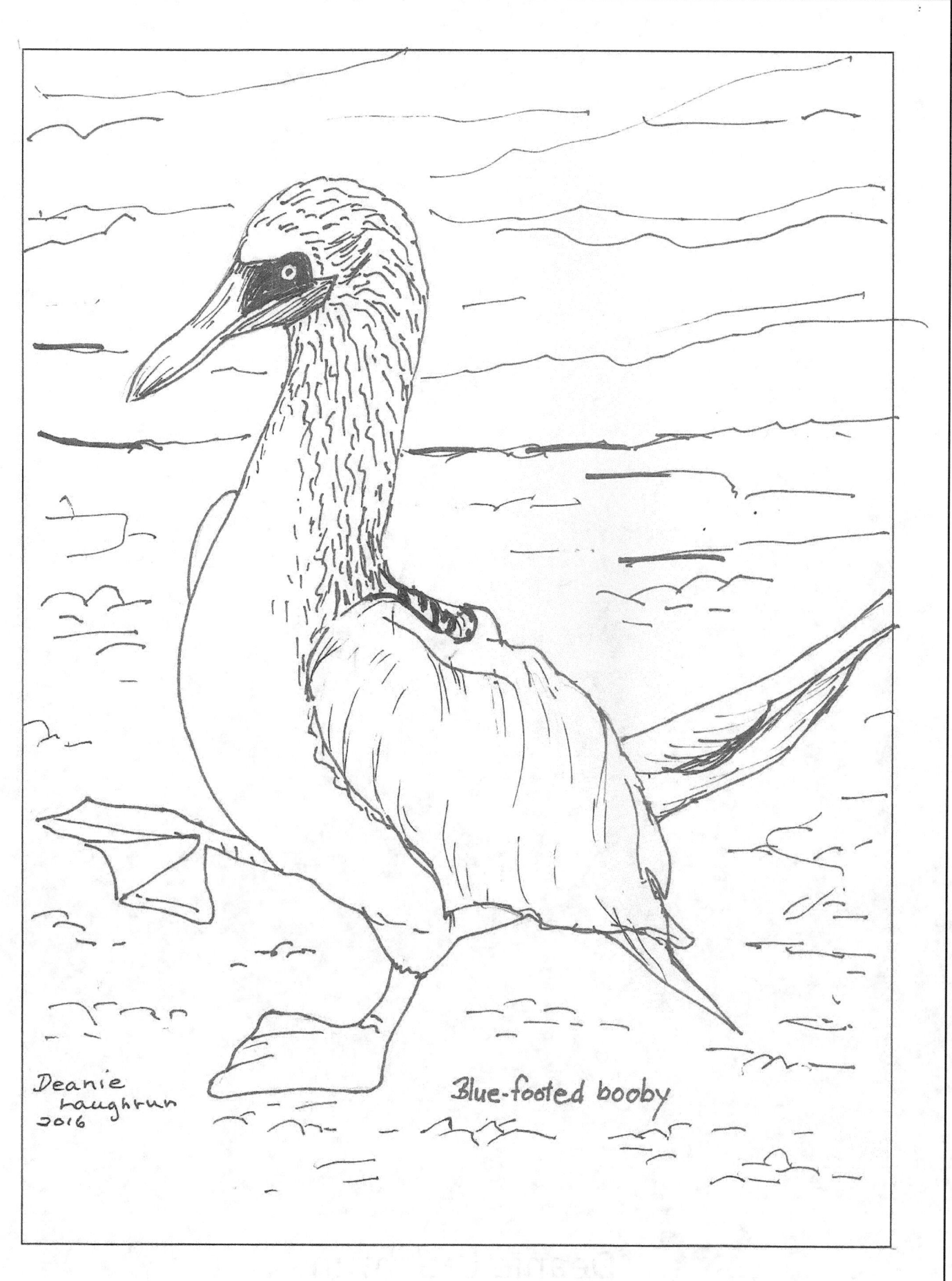

Deanie
Laughrun
2016

Blue-footed booby

Deanie Laughrun

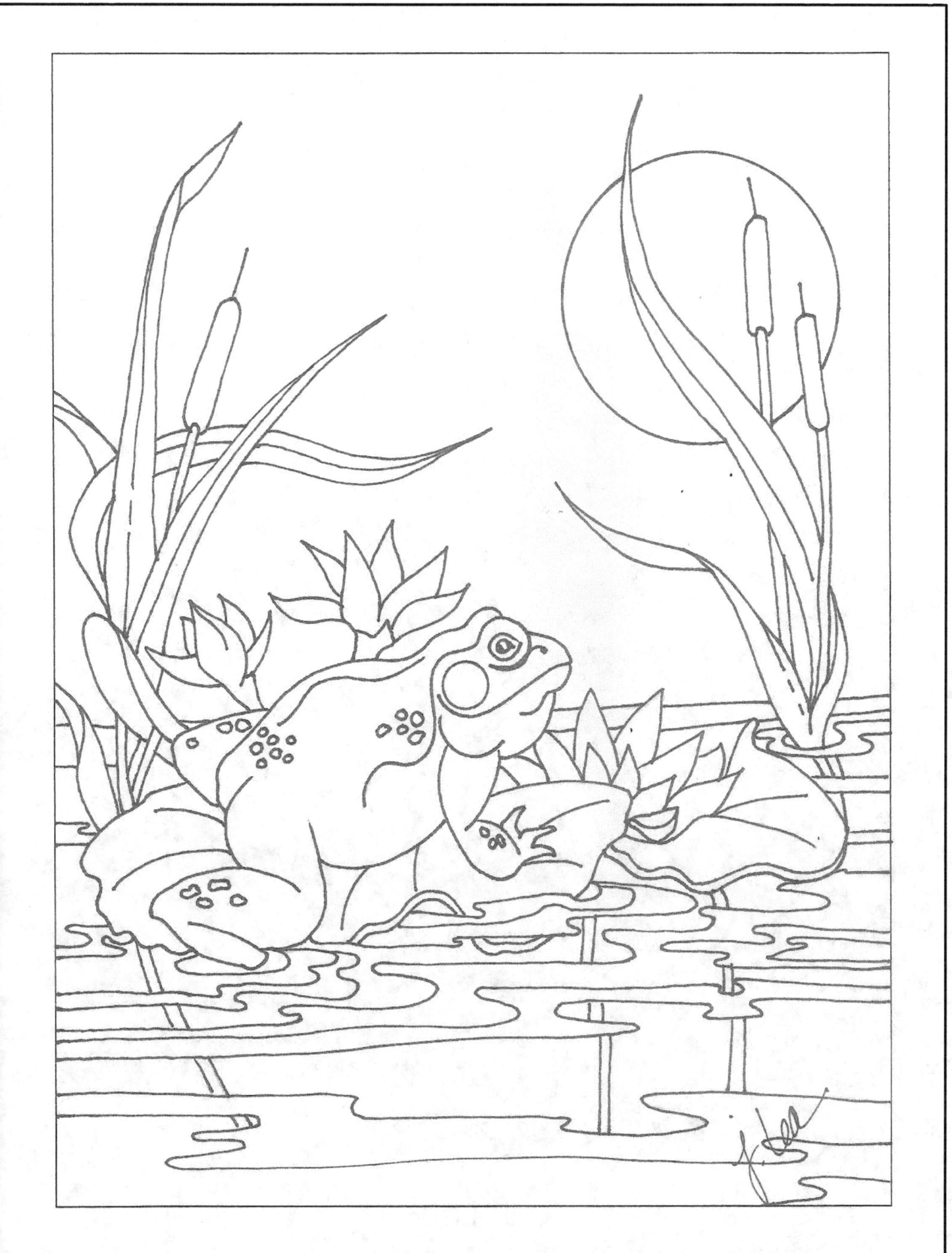

.J. Lea

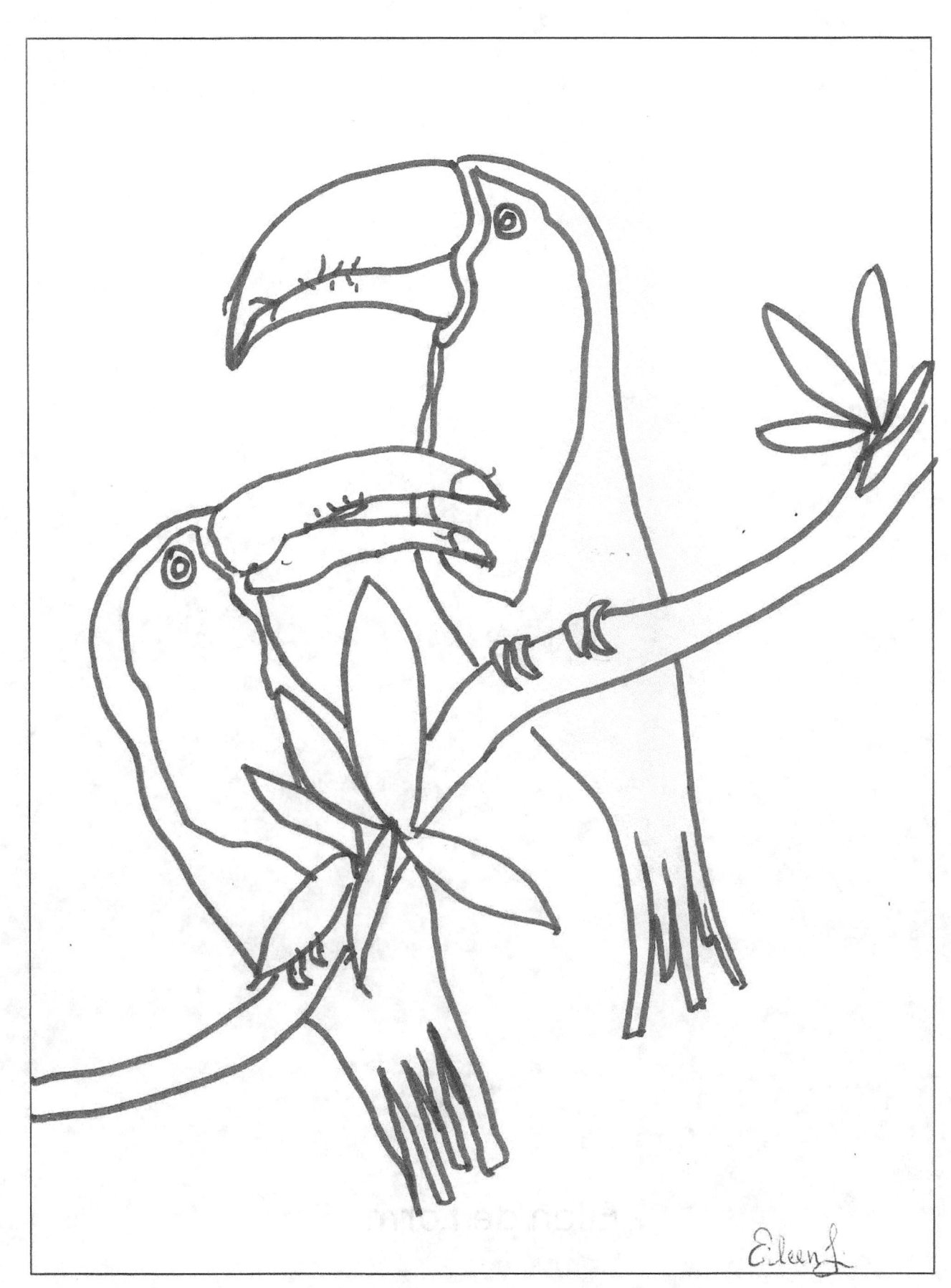

Ellen de Lorm

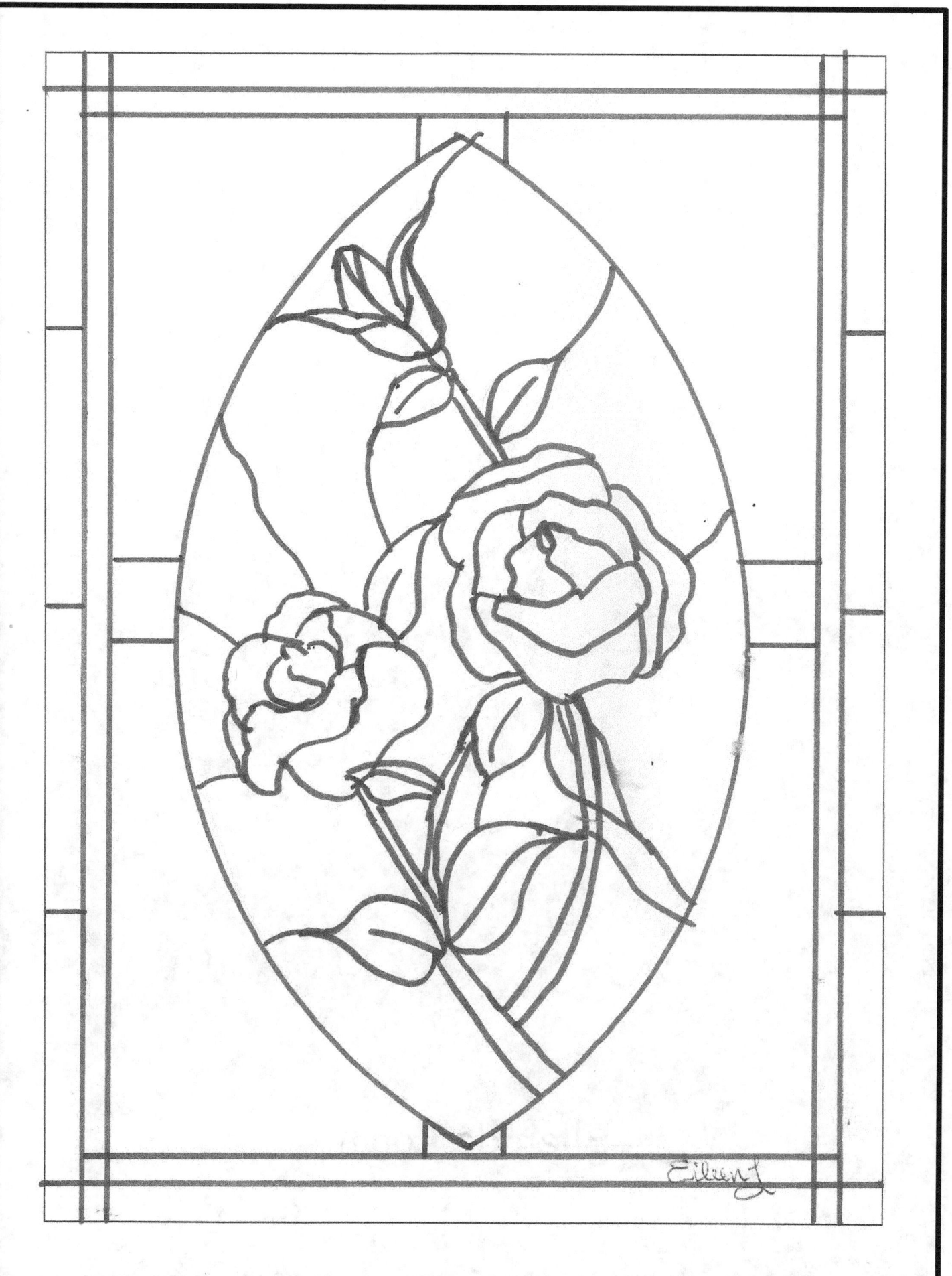

Ellen de Lorm

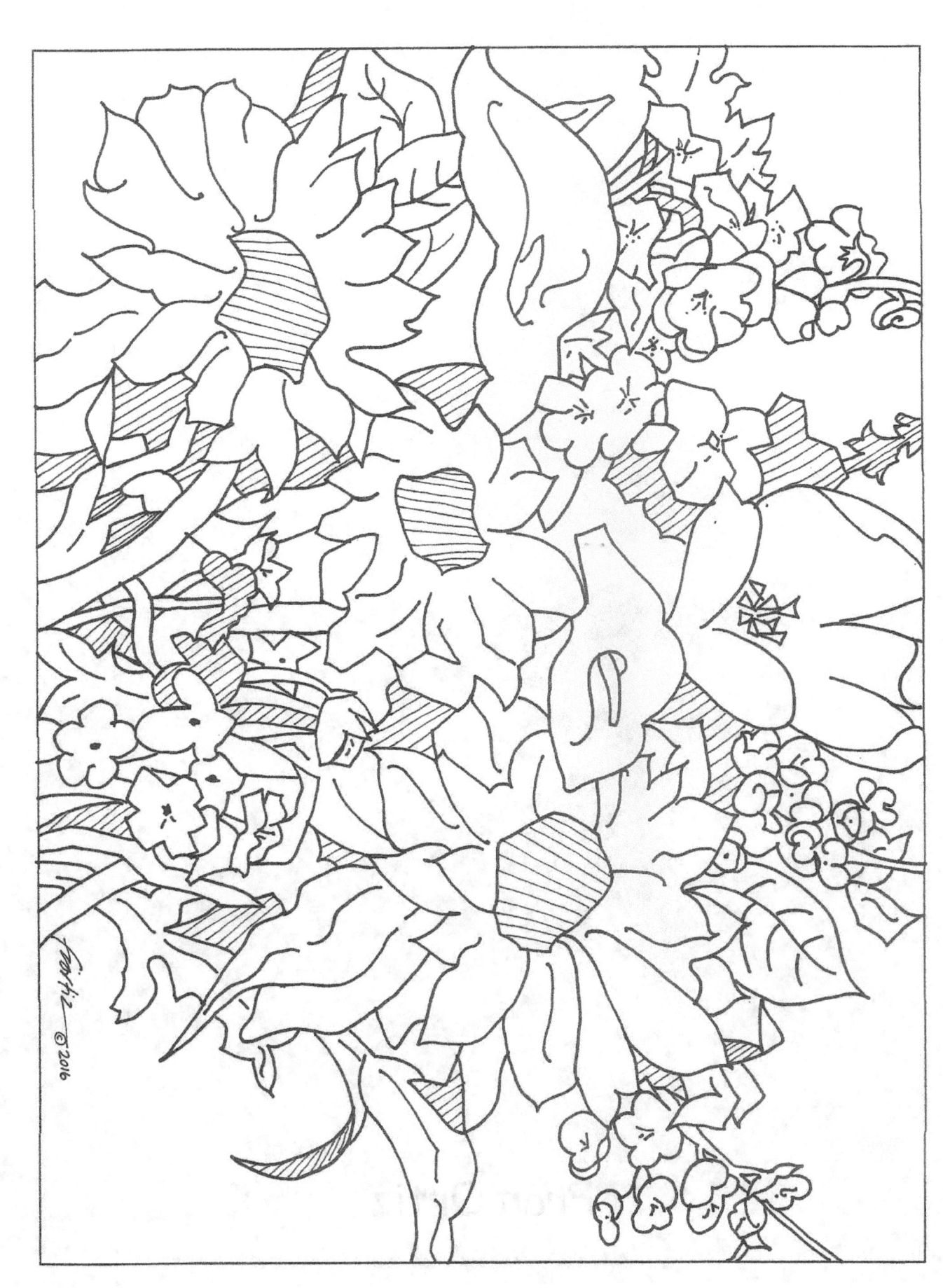

Fran Ortiz

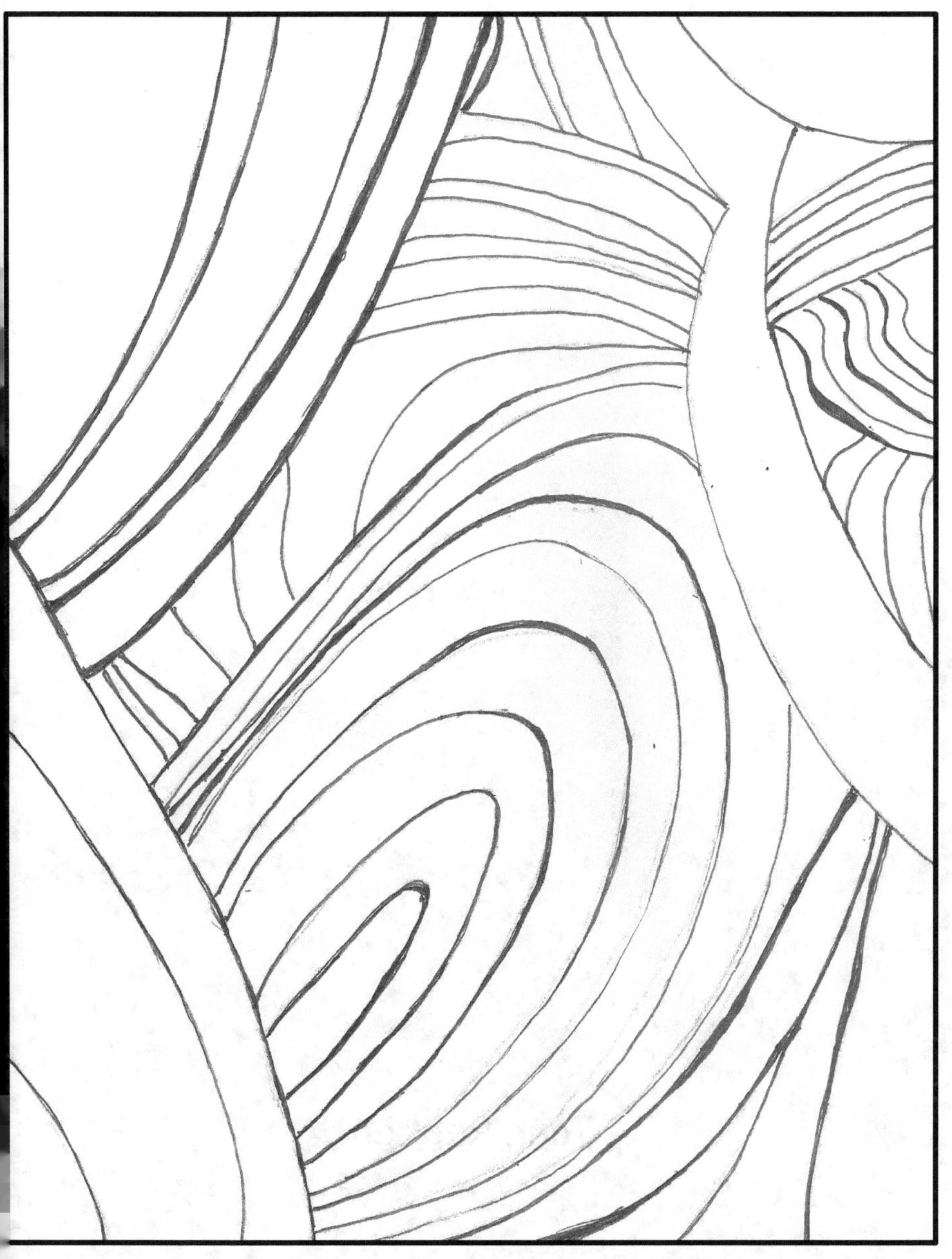

Joan Robben

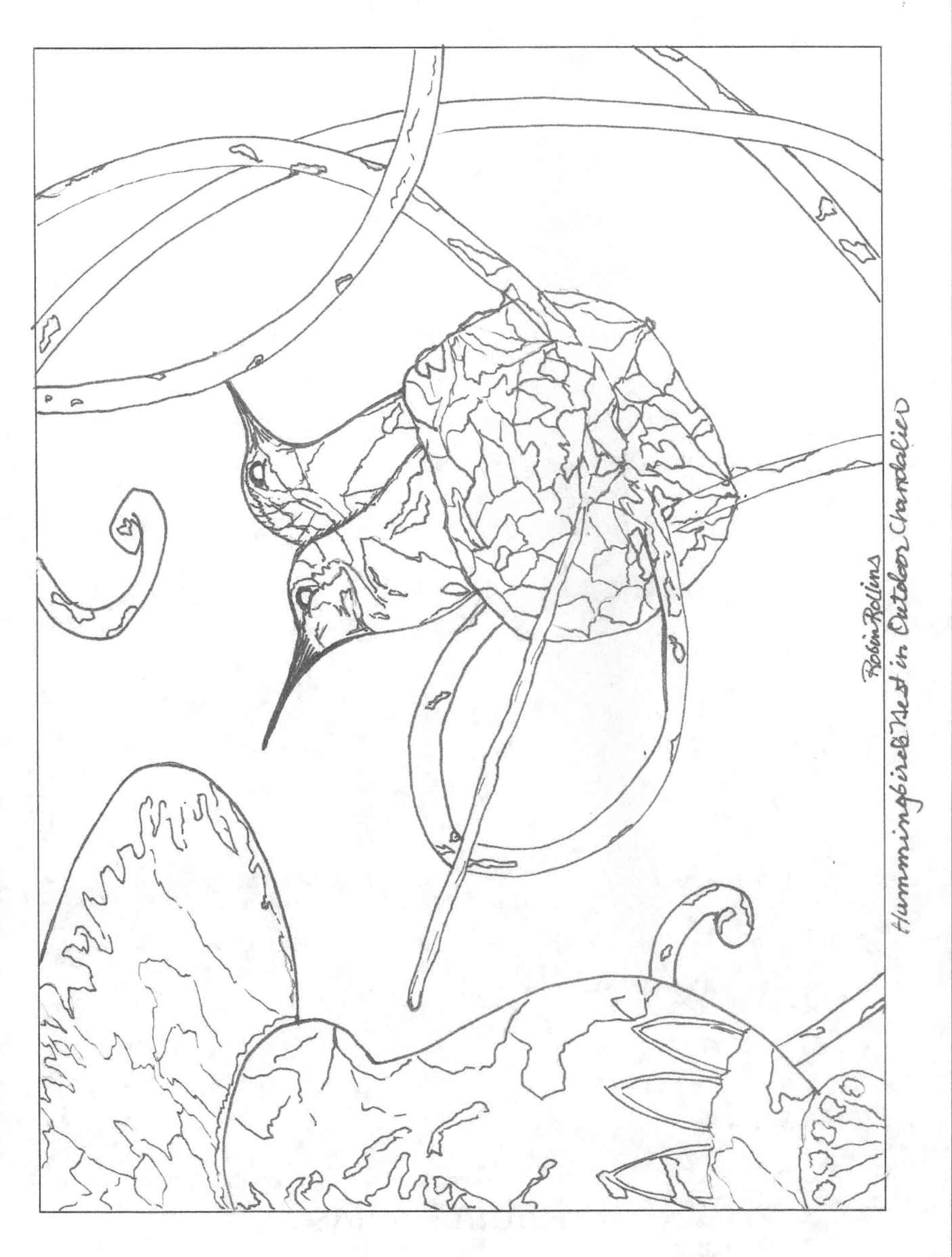

Hummingbird Nest in Outdoor Chandelier

Robin Rolins

Robin Rollins

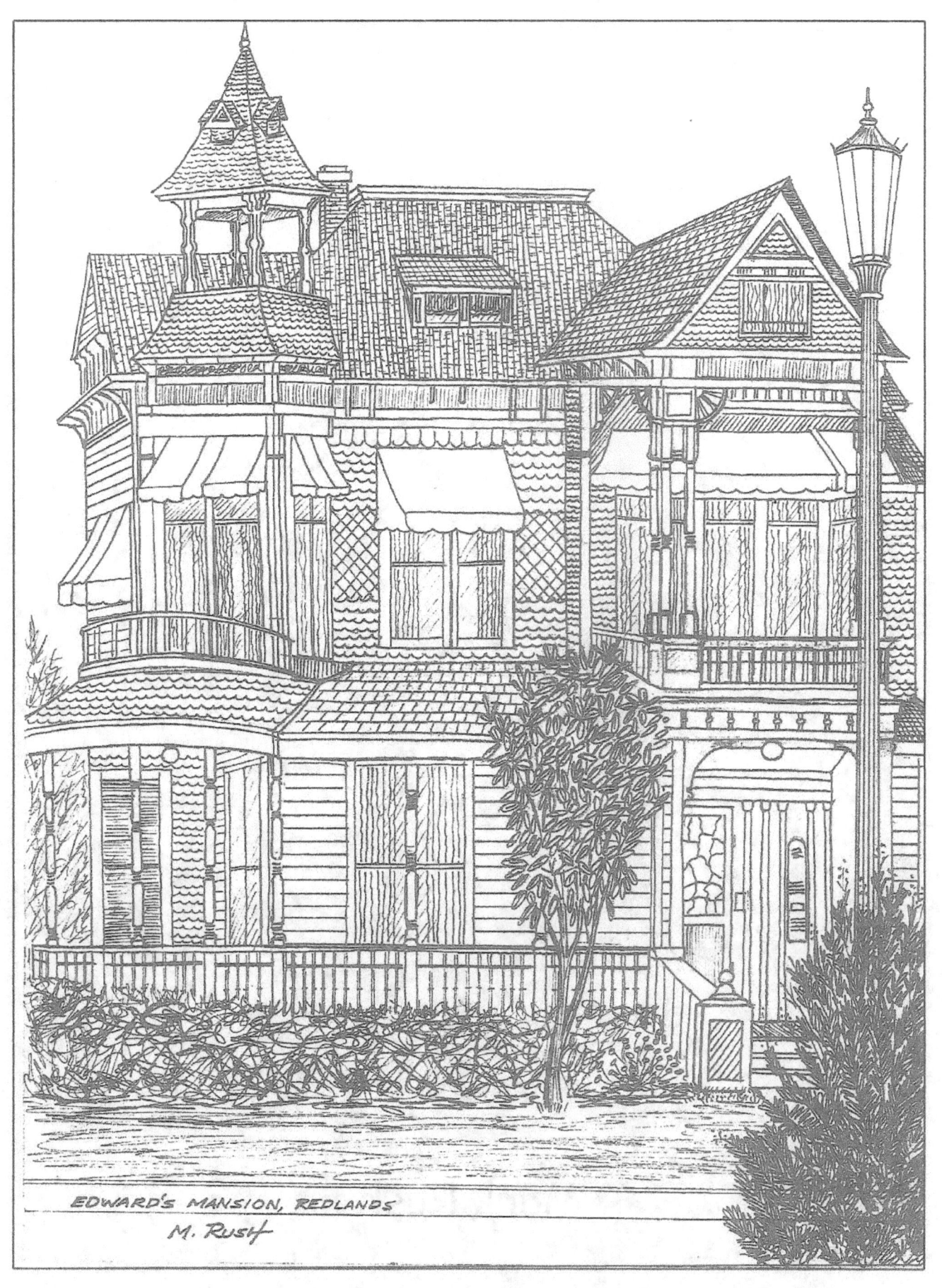

EDWARD'S MANSION, REDLANDS

M. Rush

Mark Rush

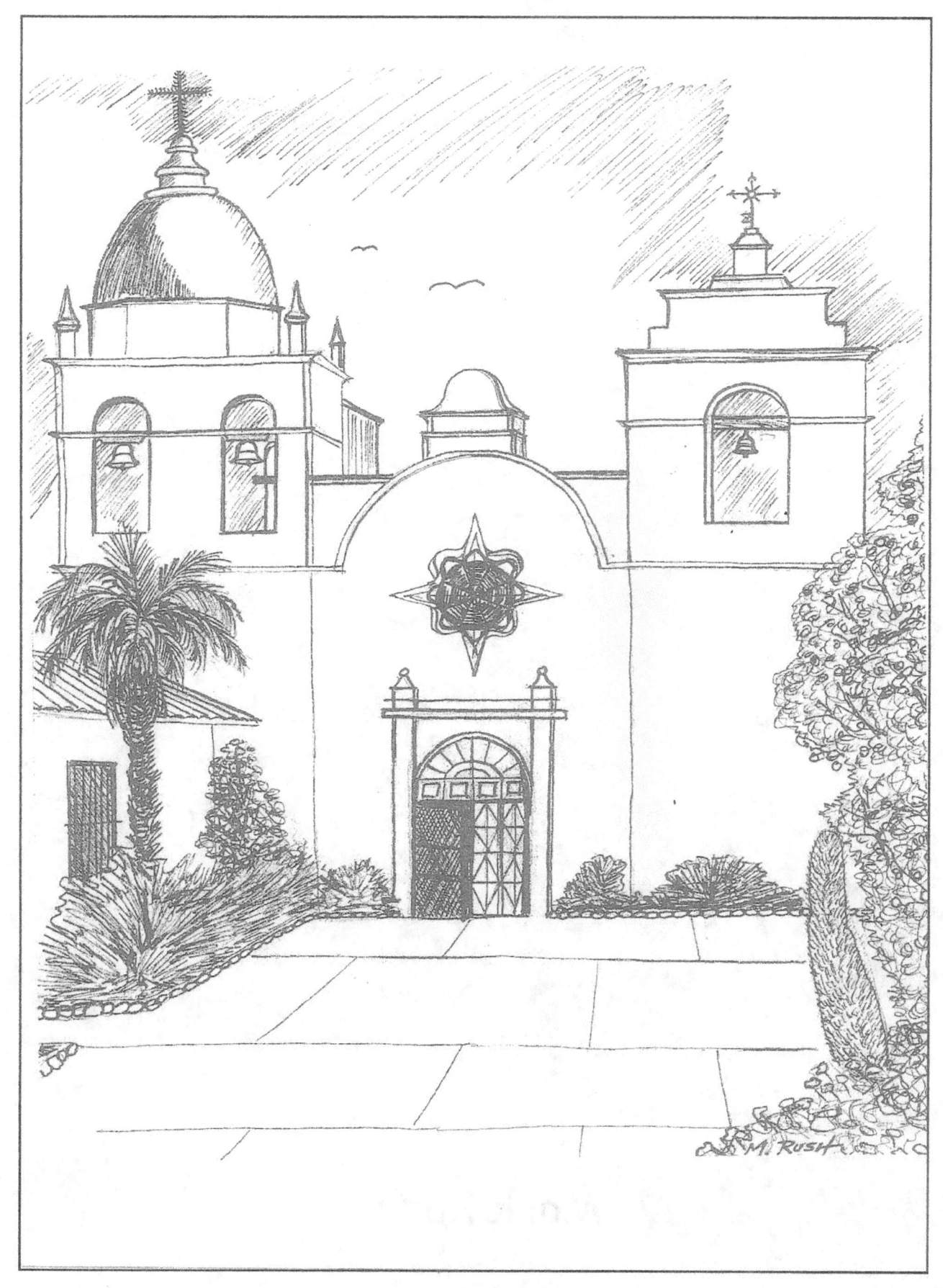

Mark Rush

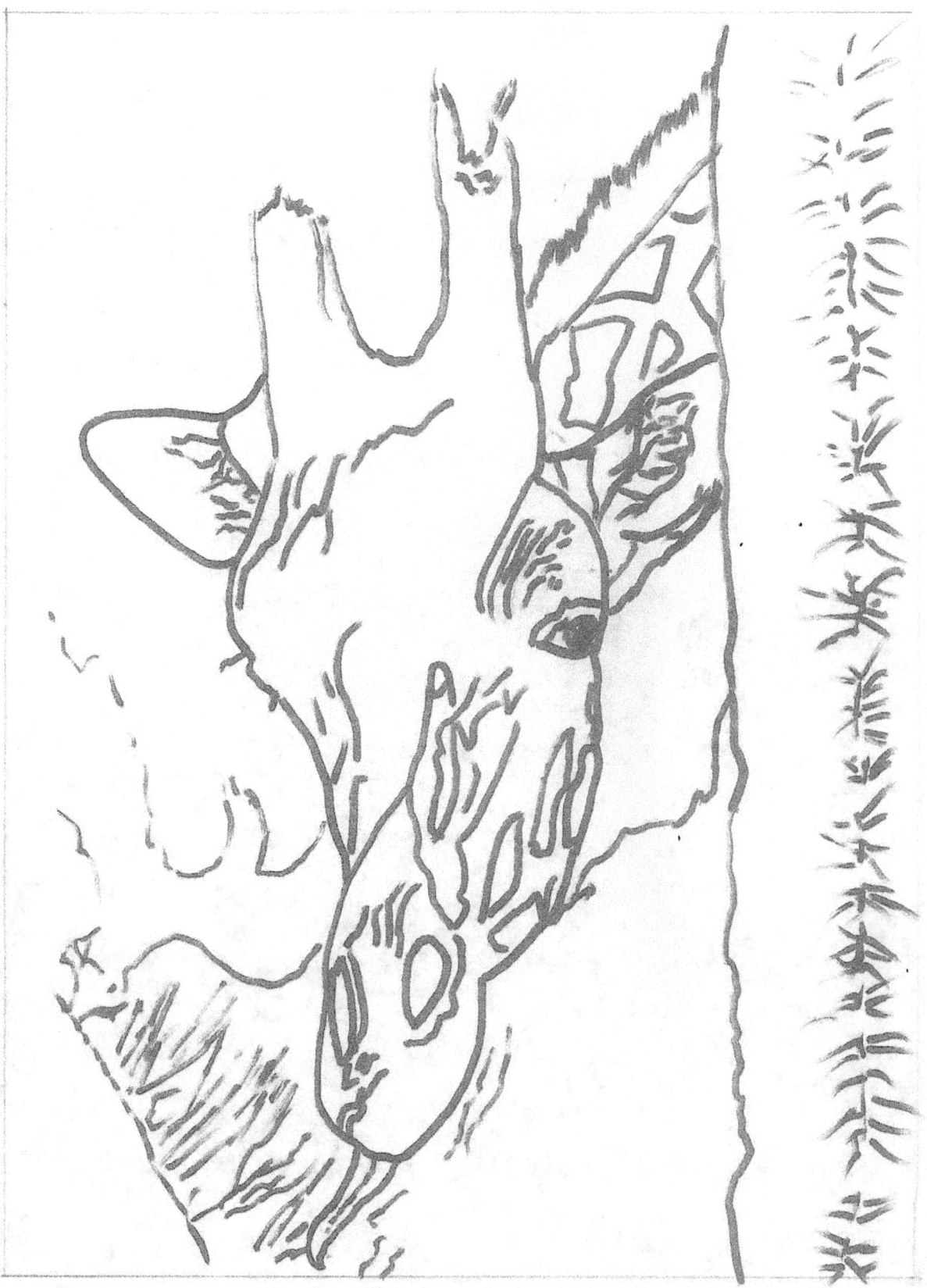

Maris Sherwood

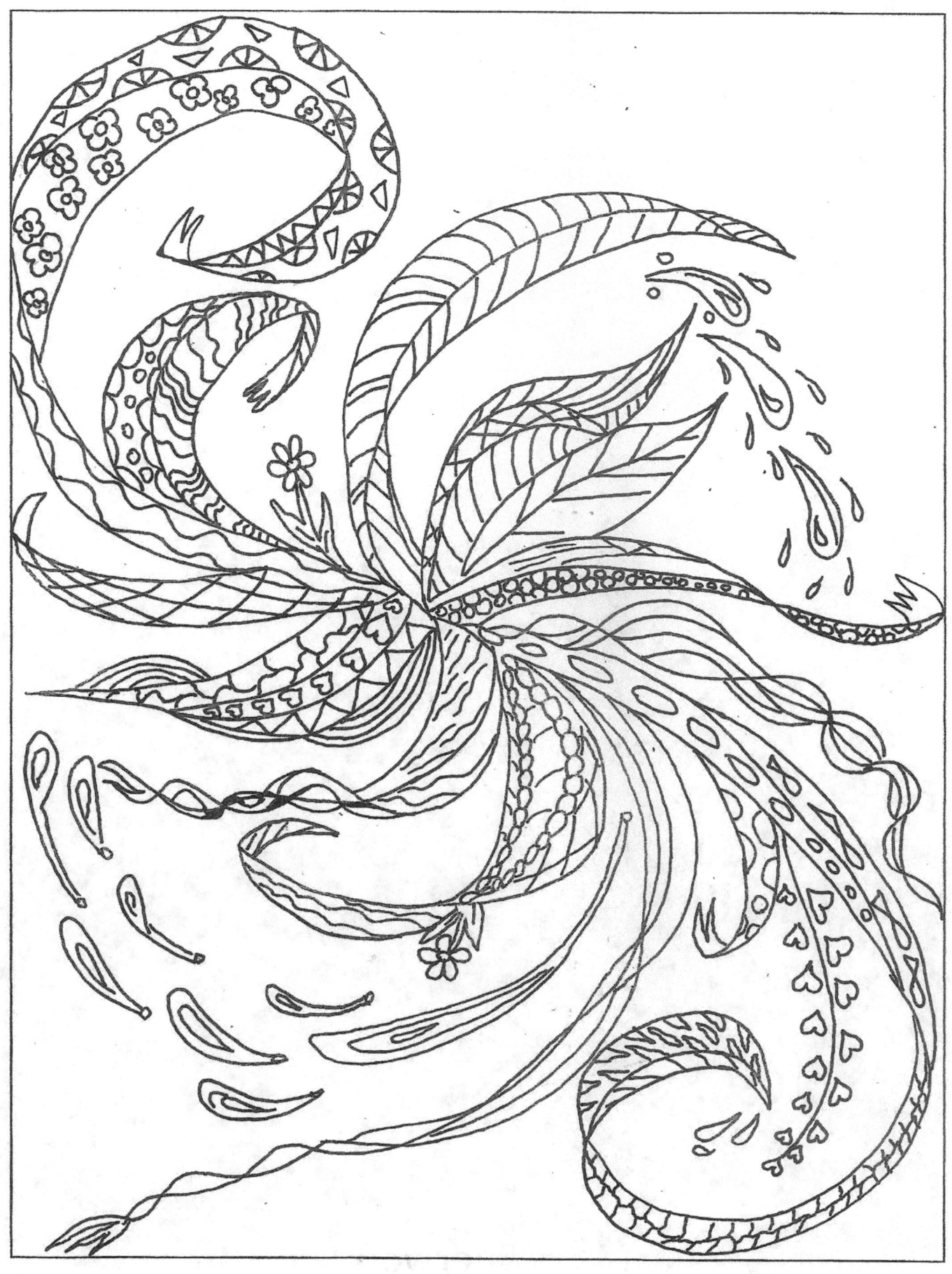

Maris Sherwood

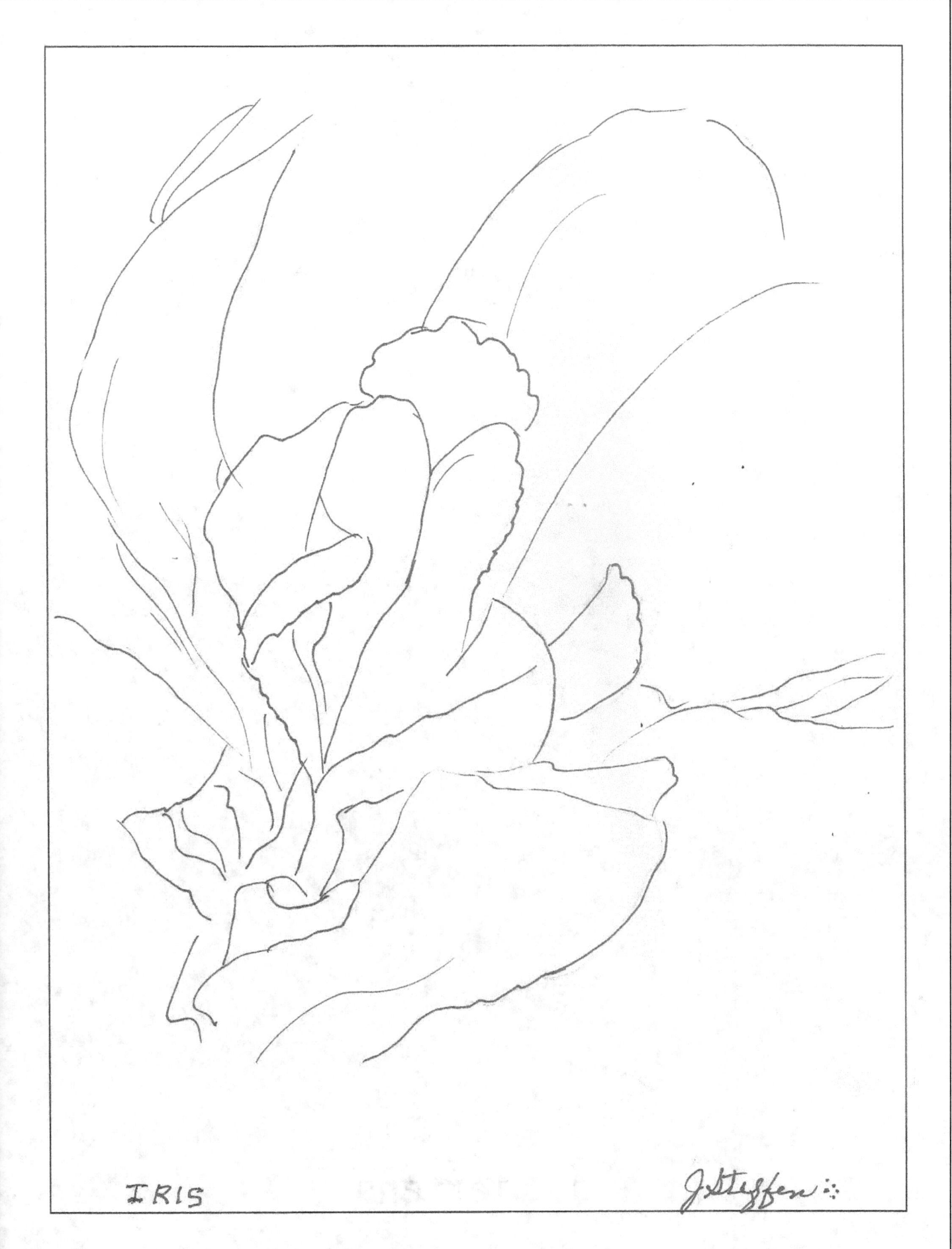

IRIS

J. Steffen

J. Steffens

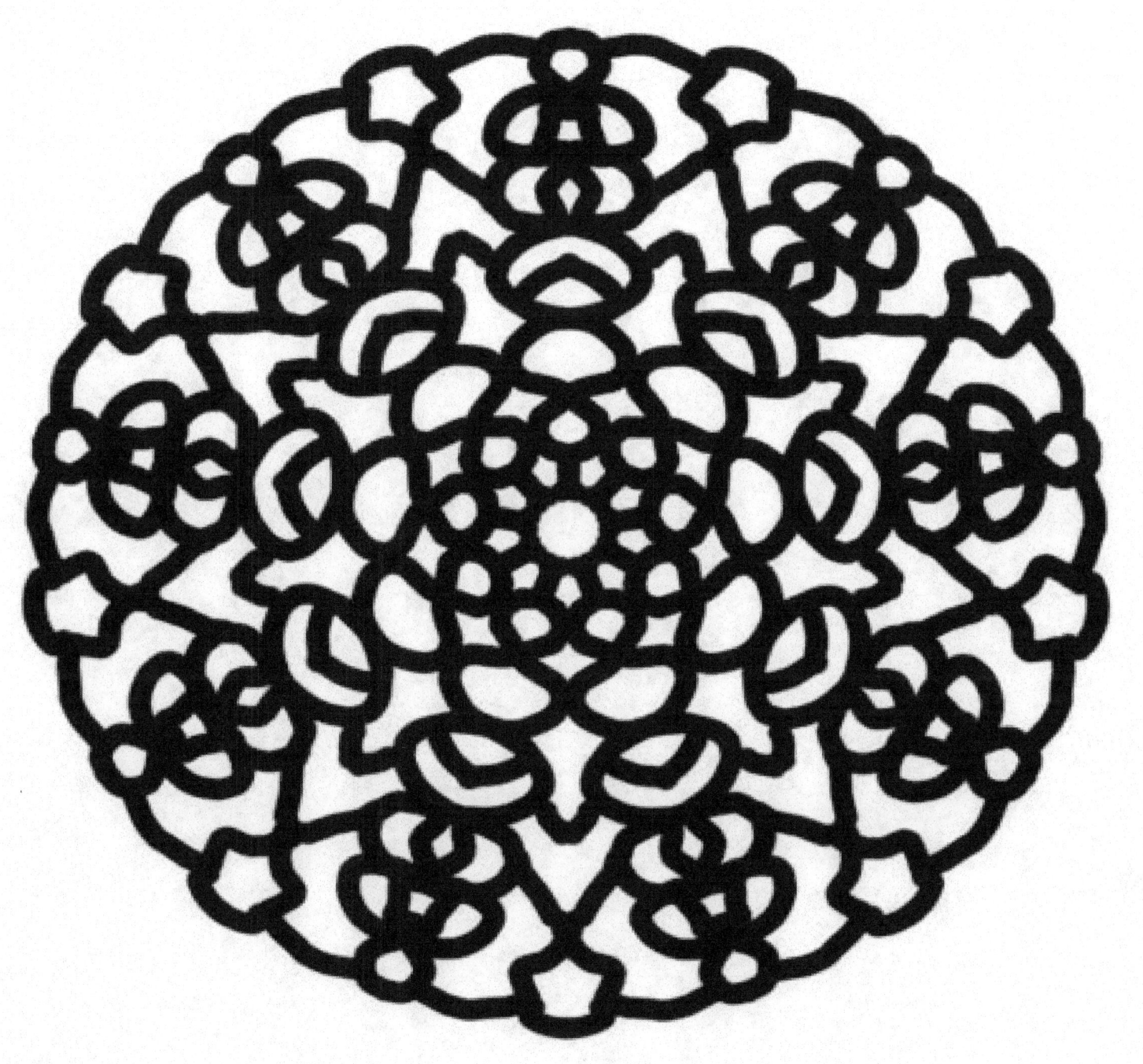

Ray Tucker

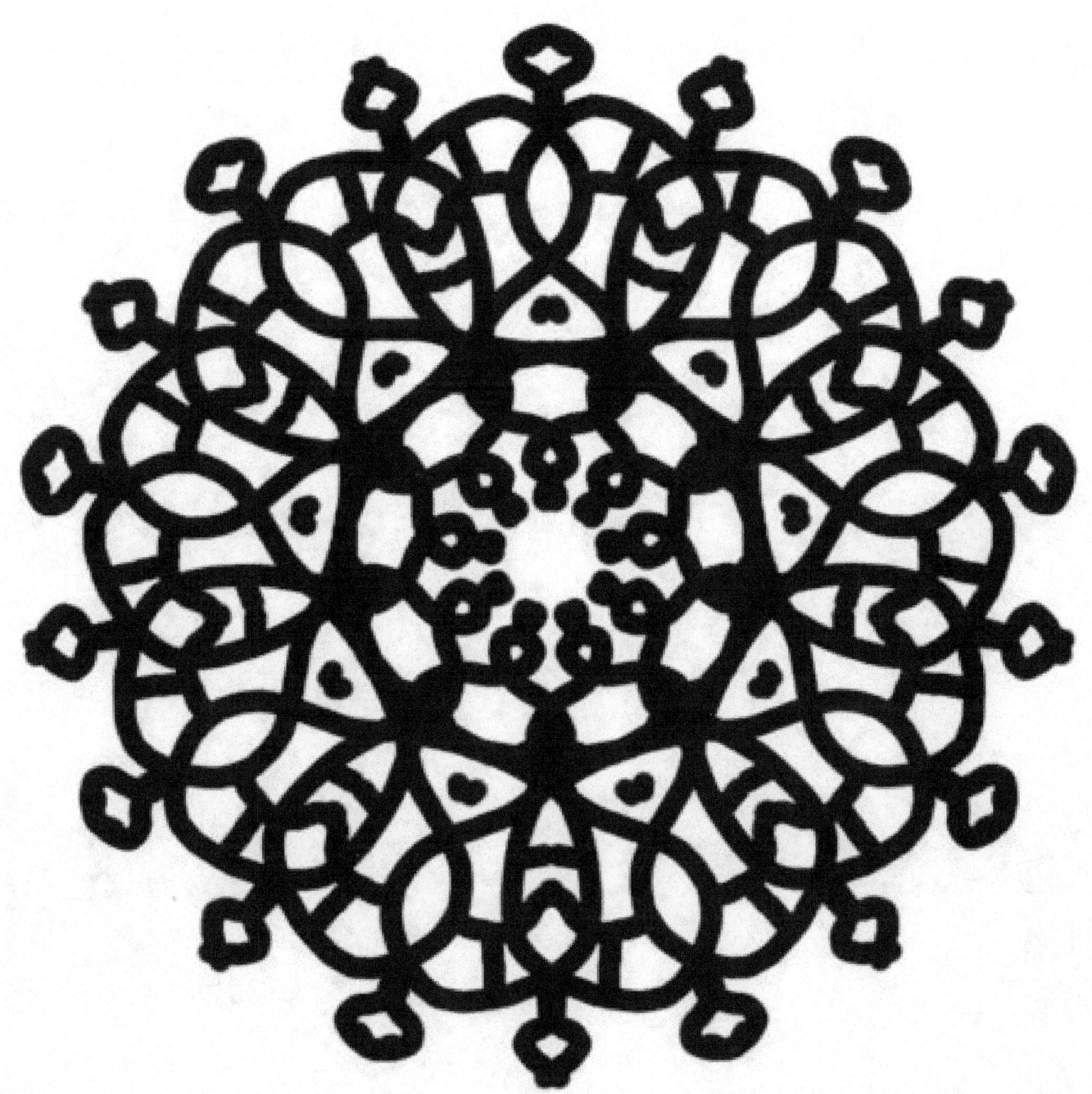

Ray Tucker

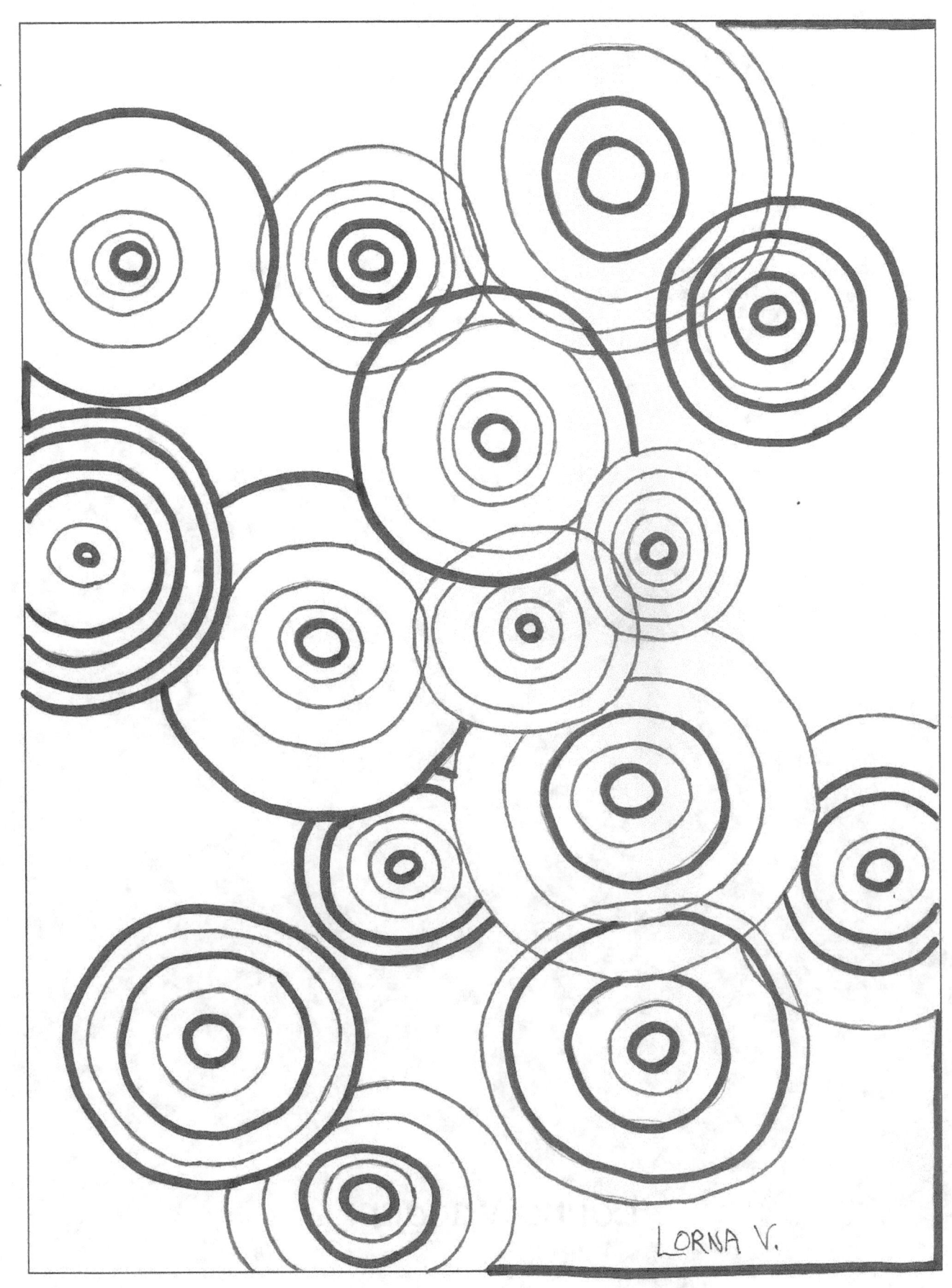

LORNA V.

Lorna Vacarri

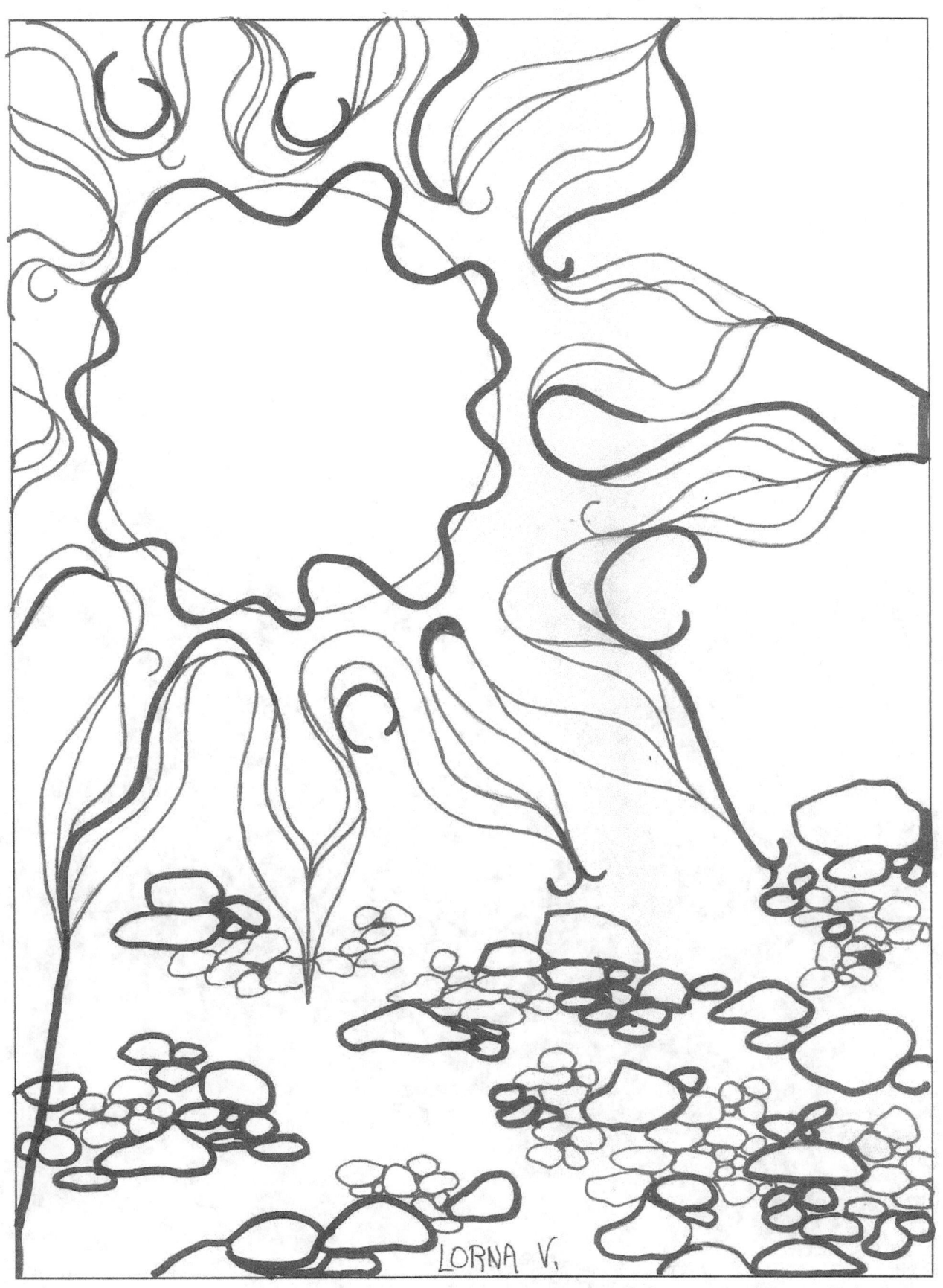

Lorna Vacarri

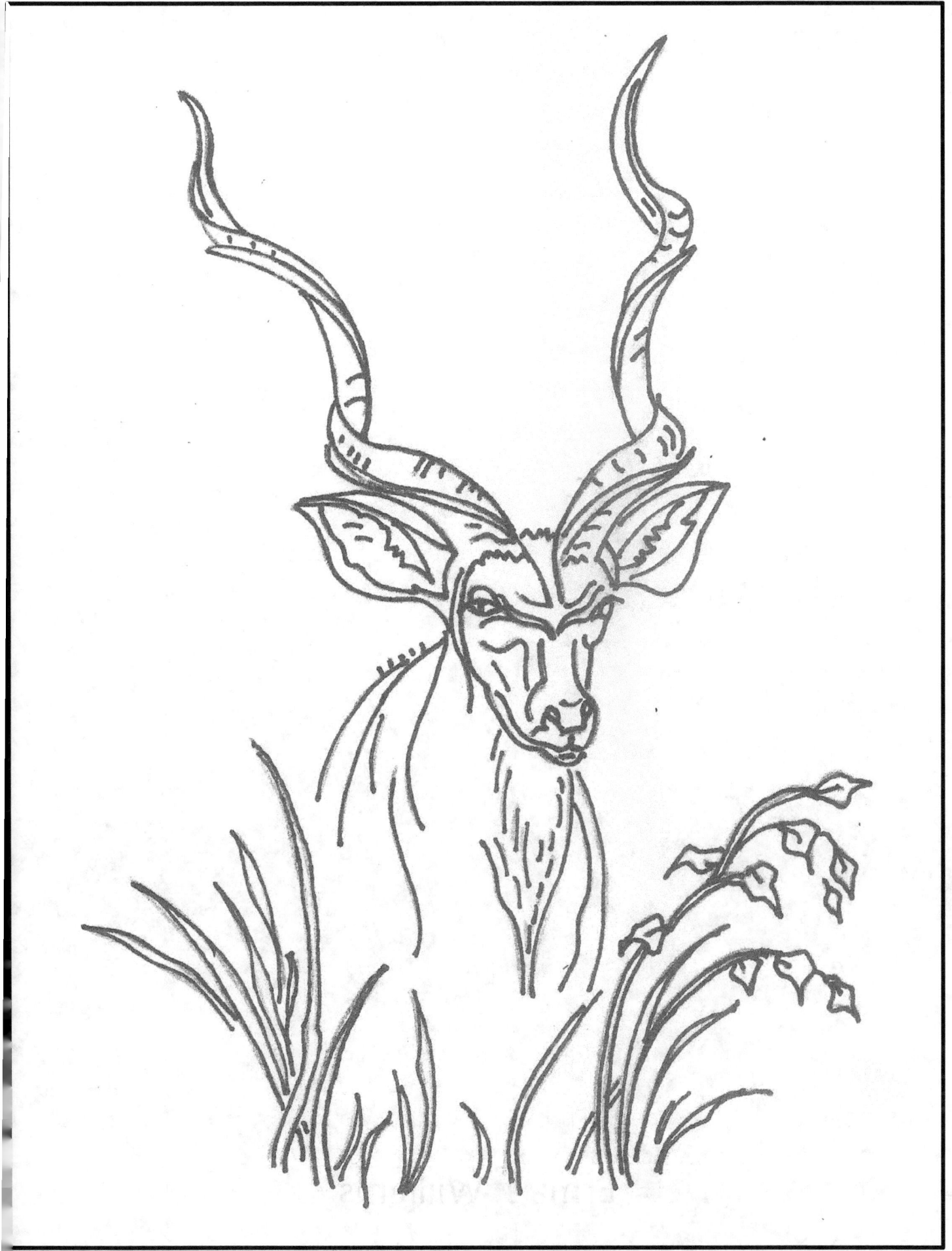

Erma J. Williams

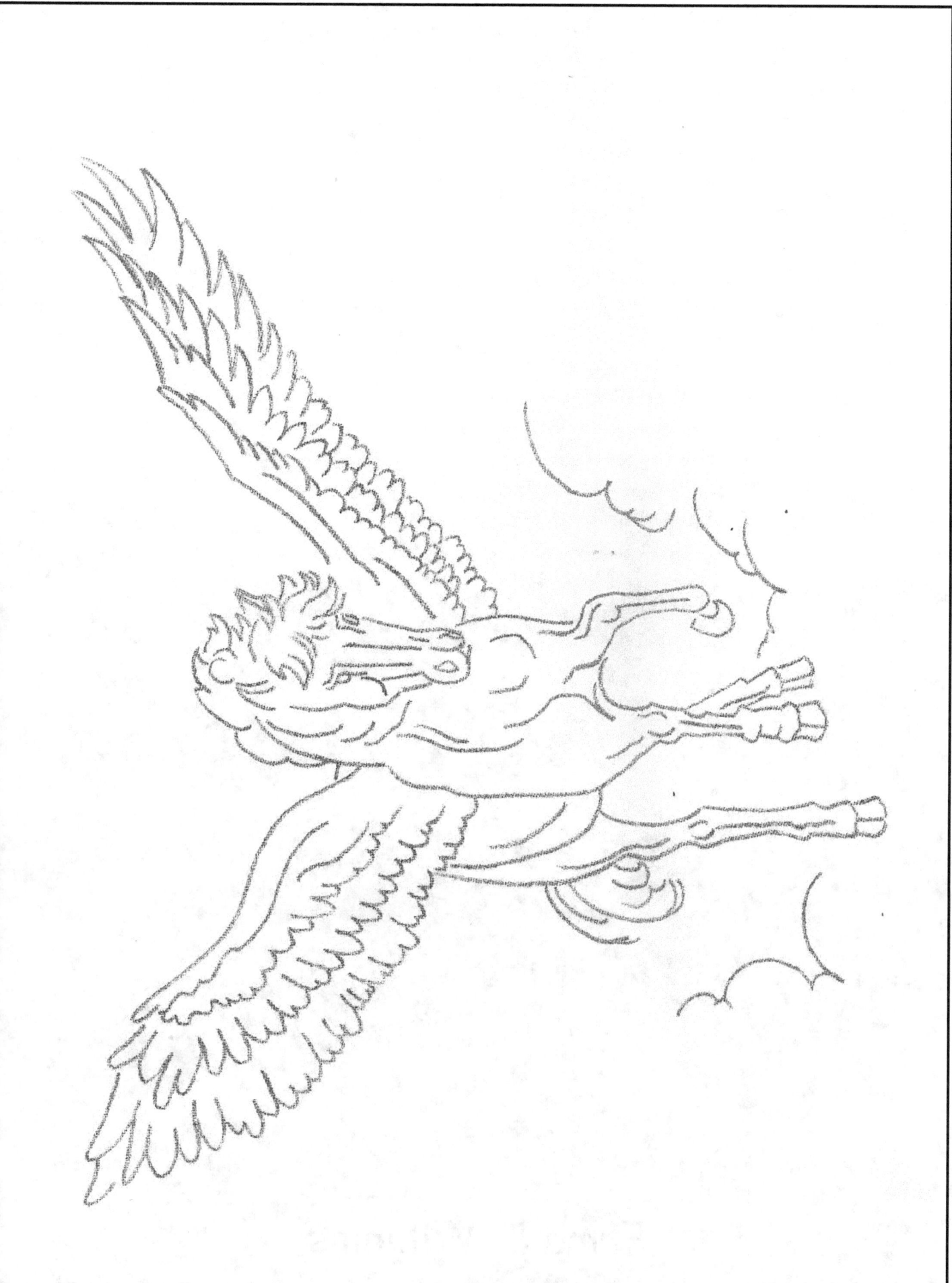

Erma J. Williams

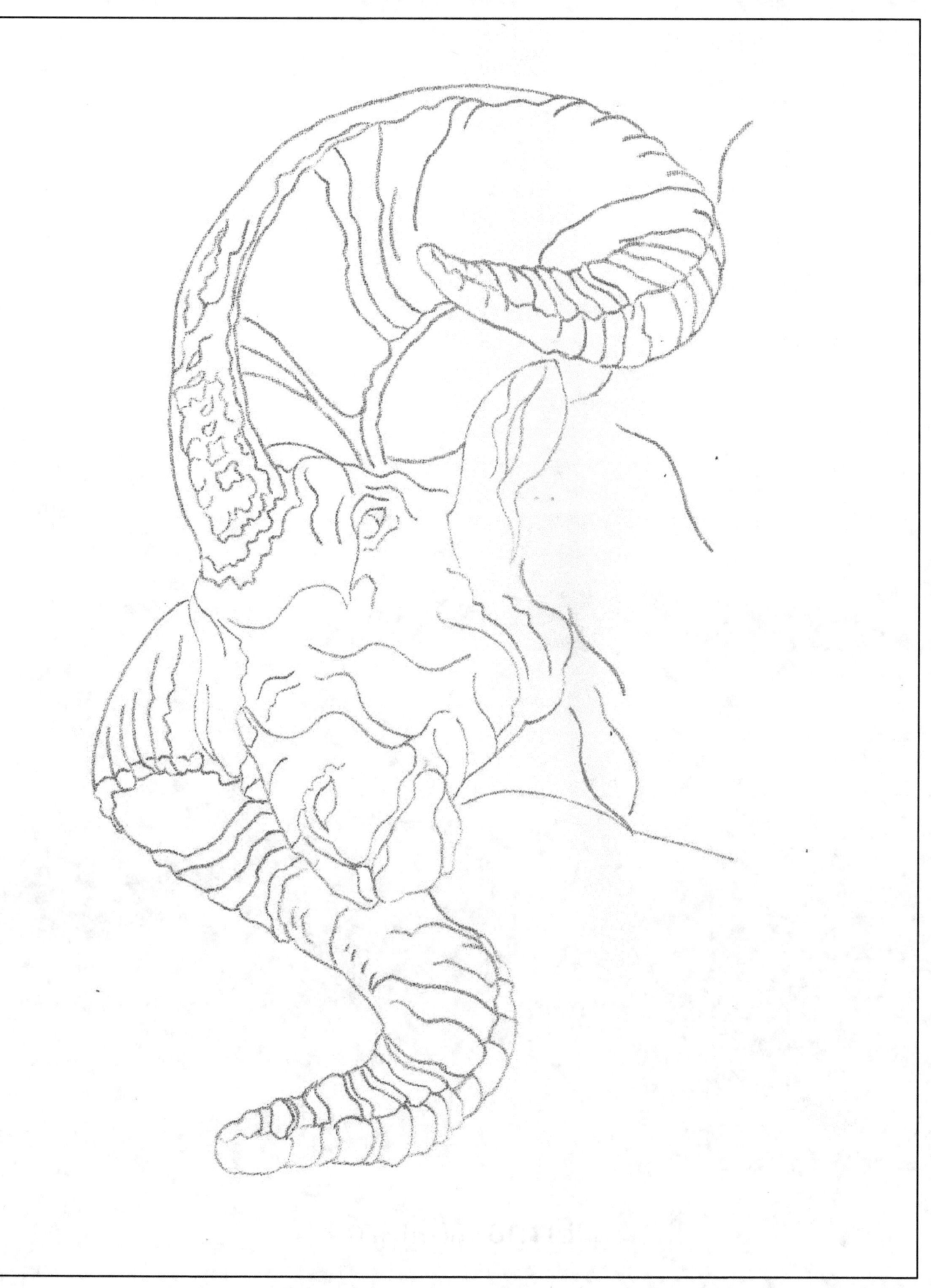

Erma Williams

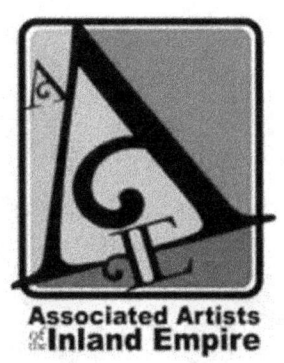

Associated Artists
of Inland Empire

This coloring book is dedicated

to all AAIE members,

past and. present,

who have helped to create one

of Southern California's finest Art Associations.

Coloring Book produced by

Ray Tucker, President AAIE

All images are the property of the artists

2016©

www.ingramcontent.com/pod-product-compliance
Lightning Source LLC
Chambersburg PA
CBHW081158180526
45170CB00006B/2135